THE POTATO COOKBOOK

Sheryl Brownlee

David Bateman

Acknowledgements

Thank you to the New Zealand Vegetable Growers' Federation Inc. for the use of their photographs and four of their recipes.

Published in 1993 David Bateman Ltd, 'Golden Heights', 32-34 View Road, Glenfield, Auckland, New Zealand

ISBN 1 86953 132 9

Cover designed by Errol McLeary
Typeset in 10/11 Helvetica 45
Printed in Hong Kong by Colorcraft Ltd

Contents

Introduction

There is probably no other vegetable in the European world that offers so much variety in the way it can be cooked and served as the potato. We probably owe this valuable tuber-bearing plant to the Spaniards who first saw it in Quito in South America in the 1540s where it was being grown by the natives. The Spaniards took it back to Spain where it was cultivated. It was first introduced into England in 1563 but its cultivation was neglected at that time and it was re-introduced in 1586 by Sir Francis Drake. (Sir Walter Raleigh is known to have cultivated potatoes on his estate near Cork in Ireland.) Over the next 100 years or so it was grown in Europe where it had a somewhat chequered career. However, by the early nineteenth century, the potato had become a staple food.

It is a suitable food for people of all ages and, in its most digestable form, namely mashed, is one of the first vegetables to be given to infants or to convalescents. Potato contains a lot of water (about 77 per cent), which is retained during the period of intestinal digestion. It therefore provides bulk and satisfies hunger easily. Weight for weight, it contains two and a half times less carbohydrate than bread. This makes it a highly desirable food for diabetics, as 40 g of bread can be replaced by 100 g of potato. It is also rich in potassium and therefore constitutes a highly alkaline food. To avoid the loss of mineral salts, in particular potassium, it should not be boiled in too much water.

Food value in a medium-sized potato, boiled in the skin and weighing 120 g, gives 3 g protein, 15 g starch, 3 g dietary fibre and 81 g water, with high traces of potassium and a smaller amount of magnesium. The vitamin C content of new potatoes is higher than in old.

The most nutritious way to eat potatoes is boiled or baked in their skin with little or no fat. The skin prevents the loss of water-soluble vitamins into the cooking water and retains fibre. Retain potato water for making soups.

The old adage "eating potatoes make you fat" is far from the truth. On its own it has very good food value, especially when boiled or baked in the skin — it is the sour cream, butter or cheese, which are high in fat, that add the calories! Frying also increases the calories, which vary with the surface area of the cut potato. The thinner the chip, the more fat is absorbed. A medium-sized boiled potato in its skin is about 80 calories; roasted in oil, the same potato provides 160 calories, but cut it into chips, that are then deep fried, and the count leaps to 240 calories.

Potatoes that are sprouting or green may contain a high level of solanine which, if eaten, can cause vomiting, diarrhoea and headaches.

This versatile vegetable has been ignored for a long time; it deserves much more credit than it is normally attributed.

Sweet potato (or kumara)

The origins of the sweet potato are clouded. Many countries claim they were among the first to cultivate this sweet-tasting tuber. Maori legend has Kupe bringing a type of sweet potato to Aotearoa in the 10th century. New England whalers are said to have established the first sweet potato crops in South Australia and Tasmania. Although called sweet potato, this vegetable, apart from being a tuber, claims little resemblance to the ordinary potato. It has little protein value, but is a good source of starch and is easily digested.

There are many varieties — some with a golden brown skin have a golden or pale orange flesh. Those with a deep reddish purple skin have a whiter flesh.

General information

Which potato to buy

Nowadays there are many different types of potatoes available. However, not so long ago, shopkeepers only advertised the potato by the area in which it was grown. Hence we had Pukekohe Potatoes (South Auckland), Oamaru Potatoes (South Island), Tasmanian potatoes etc. It is far more important to actually know the *variety,* as not all potatoes bake, fry or mash in the same way. Listed are some of the more common varieties, and remember that new cultivars are being developed each year.

Desiree — red skinned, with yellow flesh. Very good for baking, boiling, and salads.
Ilam Hardy — white flesh, good for microwaving, baking, boiling and mashing.
Iwa — best for boiling whole, bakes well.
Jersey Bennes — a smaller potato, suitable for boiling and baking.
Red Pontiac — red skin, even shape; a good all-round potato.
Rua — a good all-round, heavy-cropping potato.
Russet Burbank — red-brown skin, white flesh, excellent for chips and used throughout the world by McDonalds fast food outlets for their French fries. Also good for boiling and baking.

Sebago — white skin and flesh, oval shaped; excellent for frying, good for baking, mashing and salads.

When buying, choose carefully. Look for potatoes that are an even shape, free of blemishes, cuts, sprouting, and green patches. Remember, any green patches should be cut out, as they can prove toxic as well as giving the potato a bitter taste.

Get to know the different types of potatoes (see above). If the brand is not labelled, ask. As mentioned previously, very often the potato is named according to the area in which it was grown and not by its type.

Read the signs advertising potatoes. A common sign that can fool the consumer is "Fresh Dug Potatoes". This may be true — the potatoes are probably *just* dug — but that does not mean they are new. In fact, those particular potatoes could have been ground-stored for 6-9 months after maturing.

Fresh, new potatoes have a very thin paper-like skin, which is easily rubbed off with the fingers. Dirt adhering to potatoes is often due to the weather conditions when the potatoes were harvested. Remember, the grower cannot always harvest in ideal conditions, but consumers do expect produce all year.

Over the last few years, the packaging of potatoes has improved immensely. Sugar bags of potatoes are disappearing, and the smaller paper bags from 5 to 10 kg are more in demand. Plastic bags do nothing for the keeping quality of the potato; they actually make the potato sweat badly and also allow light to penetrate.

Growers' names are now shown on the bags or labels, and some producers are also stamping the brand of potato on the bags as well. Gourmet packs are also available and this is a great way to sample small quantities of unfamiliar types.

Washed potatoes are also prominently displayed and many consumers find the price difference is well worth this extra service.

Storage

Regardless of where you purchase your potatoes, or when you lift them from the garden, storage is most important. To stop greening (as mentioned earlier), they should be removed from plastic bags and kept in a dry, dark place. Dampness and light will certainly destroy the potato.

Hints on preparing and cooking potatoes

Remember that different types of potatoes take varying times to cook. Floury ones are excellent for boiling and mashing; the waxy potato is great for frying and potato salads. Times given are approximate only.

Preparation

Too often the potato is over cooked, boiled to a mush, and then the comment is made, "What shocking potatoes these are", whereas, in fact, with a little careful handling, excellent results can be achieved. New potatoes should only need a light scrub to remove dirt. Cut out any blemishes. Older potatoes may need peeling and any eyes removed. Also ,cut large potatoes in half before peeling to make sure they are sound in the middle.

Peel potatoes as thinly as possible as vitamins and minerals are stored in and just below the skin.

For even cooking, cut, slice or dice potatoes into evenly-sized pieces.

Baking/roasting

Prepare potatoes as above. Place on a rack or in a baking dish. If they are brushed with a little cooking oil, they will cook more quickly than if left dry. Sprinkling salt and pepper over the skin intensifies the flavour. Potatoes can be parboiled and rolled in flour before baking.

Vegetables roasted in the oven with meat require little attention. Make sure that the fat is bubbling or it will be absorbed into the potato. They will need to be turned every 10–15 minutes. If the meat has nearly finished cooking, it may be better to remove it from the oven (keep it covered) and bake the potatoes separately. Return the meat to the oven for the last 15-20 minutes; this should prevent it from overcooking. Potatoes baked or roasted in the oven should take about 40–60 minutes at 200°C.

Another method is to lightly brush the skins with butter, wrap the whole potato in tinfoil, then bake in the oven.

Boiling

Peel if necessary, and place cut, diced or sliced potatoes in just enough water to cover them. Bring slowly to the boil, add salt if required, and cook until just tender; about 12–20 minutes. Do not discard the cooking water — keep it for soups or gravies as it contains important nutrients, especially if the potatoes are cooked in their skins.

Deep frying

Slice or chip the potatoes to the desired thickness (thinner slices will cook more quickly). Soak for at least 10 minutes in cold water to remove excess starch. Dry thoroughly as any water left on can make the oil splatter badly. Preheat oil to 190°C. Place a small quantity of chips in a chip basket and lower carefully into the hot oil.

Cook for 5–8 minutes, drain well. Increase the oil temperature again and add the next batch. Continue in this way until all the chips have been fried. Now they need to be deep fried in batches again for 3–5 minutes and drained well. The second frying crisps and browns the outer skin, and can be done just before serving. If too many chips are placed in the basket, the temperature of the oil will drop and it will be absorbed into the chips.

Microwaving

The smaller the amount or number of potatoes microwaved at one time, the quicker the cooking process.

Whole potatoes must be pricked with a fork to lessen the chances of them exploding while cooking. They should be placed around the outer edge of a plate to ensure more even cooking. A medium potato may cook in 3–4 minutes, but four potatoes may take 15–20 minutes. The wattage of the microwave will also alter the cooking time.

The cooking process will be speeded up if holes are made by pushing a metal skewer through the potato in two or three different places before cooking. It breaks up the density of the potato, allowing the microwaves to penetrate and cook more quickly.

After microwaving, allow potatoes to stand for at least a third of the cooking time before eating.

To increase the colour on the outer skin of microwaved potatoes, brush with a combination of soy sauce and honey, or with one of the many commercial products that are now available for browning.

Sliced or diced potatoes should be evenly-sized, and placed in a wide-based dish. Add a small amount of salted water, cover with a lid or microwave film and cook on high power for 5–9 minutes, depending on the quantity, and the wattage of the microwave. *Note*: If salt is used when microwaving potatoes, it is easier to dissolve it in water before adding it to the dish, rather than sprinkling it on during cooking.

For mashed potatoes, peel and evenly chop or dice 500–700 g potatoes. Place in a microproof bowl or jug, add ½–1 t salt, ½ c milk, and a knob of butter. Cover and microwave on high power (100%) for 5 minutes. Stir, cover, and microwave a further 5–8 minutes or until tender. Stand covered for at least 5 minutes, or until just before serving, then mash, adjust the seasoning and serve. Do not mash immediately as heat is lost during mashing, and the potatoes are more difficult to reheat.

Microwave and roasting

By using both methods, the overall cooking time is reduced. Depending on the size of the potato, leave whole or cut into pieces.. Place round the outer edge of a dish and microwave for 3–6 minutes. To obtain a crispy brown outer skin, shallow or deep fry for a few minutes; bake in hot oven (200°C) until the skin is brown; or place under grill, turning until crisp and brown.

Oven steaming

Scrub potatoes. Pour hot water into a pan and place potatoes on a rack over it. Cover completely and bake at 180°C for 45–60 minutes.

Pressure cooking

Scrub or peel potatoes, cut into evenly-sized pieces, add a small amount of water and cook according to the pressure cooker instructions. (These vary considerably from one type of pressure cooker to another.) This method takes about one third of the cooking time it takes to boil potatoes.

Note: If potatoes blacken during cooking, this may be caused by a reaction between chlorengic acid and iron. This reaction is affected by the potato variety, the amount of iron in the soil in which the tuber was grown, or the water it is cooked in. To overcome this, squeeze lemon juice into the cooking water at the start of cooking.

Freezing

To freeze potatoes, peel, wash and cut into chips. Plunge into boiling water for 2 minutes, rinse thoroughly in cold water, dry well, pack into plastic bags and freeze.

Chips prepared in this way will keep in the freezer for up to three months.

Notes to remember when using this cookbook

Due to the many different types of potatoes and sweet potatoes that are available, I have tried to identify them only as new or old.

1 c equals a level 250 ml cup
1 T equals 1 metric tablespoon
1 t equals 1 metric teaspoon

Salt. The amount of salt used is not usually stated as this is very much a question of preference. Add as much or little as you wish, but remember that if stock cubes are used in a recipe instead of stock, less salt may be required.

Servings. The number of servings is an indication only, and often depends on what is accompanying the dish. Also, the weather and time of the day will often determine the amount of food one person can eat.

Cooking: Sweet potatoes can be cooked in the same way as potatoes, and many of the recipes are interchangeable.

Soups

Carrot and potato soup

(serves 5–6)

50 g butter
4–5 medium carrots, peeled and chopped
4 medium potatoes, peeled and chopped
1 onion, peeled and sliced
salt and pepper
1 T sugar
6 c chicken stock (or water and stock cubes)
2–3 T finely chopped parsley

Melt butter in a large frying pan or saucepan. Add carrots, potatoes and onion, sauté gently, season with salt and pepper, add sugar. Cover and cook gently for 10 minutes, shaking the pan occasionally. Add stock, bring to the boil, then simmer for 15 minutes or until the vegetables are tender.

Remove $\frac{1}{2}$–1 c drained vegetables and set aside. Purée or blend the remaining mixture until smooth. Finely chop the reserved vegetables, add to soup and reheat gently (do not boil). Adjust seasoning and stir in parsley. Serve immediately.

Kumara and orange soup

(serves 5–6)

600 g kumara, peeled and roughly chopped
1 onion, finely chopped
3 c chicken stock (preferably homemade)
$^1/_2$ c orange juice
1 T grated orange rind
freshly ground black pepper
1 c water
orange rind, sour cream, parsley (for garnish)

Place the kumara, onion and stock in a saucepan. Cover and simmer gently for 25–35 minutes or until the kumara is soft. Purée or blend until smooth. Add orange juice and rind, pepper and water. Add extra water if a thinner consistency is preferred. Heat and garnish.

Sweet potato Vichyssoise

(serves 6)

The delicate colour of this soup will depend on the type of kumara or sweet potato used. It can be served hot or cold.

4 T butter
4 leeks, washed and sliced
6 c chicken stock (or water and stock cubes)
1$^1/_2$ c dry white wine
4 large kumara or sweet potatoes, peeled and diced
grated rind and juice of 1 orange or lemon
1 c milk
1 c cream
salt and pepper
sour cream, freshly chopped herbs (for garnish)

Melt butter in a large saucepan, add leeks and sauté until soft and transparent. Add stock, wine and kumara. Heat until boiling, then simmer until kumara are tender; about 15 minutes. Stir in lemon or orange rind and juice, milk and cream. Season to taste. Purée or blend the soup until smooth.

Reheat gently (do not allow to boil). If serving hot, garnish as required. If serving cold, allow to cool, and then refrigerate for several hours. Add garnish just before serving.

Sweetcorn soup

(serves 6–7)

25 g butter
3–4 bacon rashers (for garnish)
1 onion, peeled and diced
1 clove garlic, peeled and chopped
1 carrot, peeled and chopped
1–2 sticks of celery, chopped
6 c chicken stock (or water and stock cubes)
4–5 medium potatoes, peeled and diced
375-g can whole kernel sweetcorn, drained
salt and pepper
3 T chopped parsley or chives

Melt butter in a large frying pan, add bacon and fry until crisp. Remove bacon and set aside. When cool, dice.

Add onion and garlic to the pan, and cook until soft. Add carrot, celery, stock, potatoes and half the sweetcorn. Bring to the boil, stir, and simmer for about 15 minutes or until the potatoes are just soft. Cool for 5 minutes, then purée or blend until smooth. Return to the pan, add salt and pepper to taste, stir in parsley or chives and remaining sweetcorn, and reheat gently. Ladle into serving dishes and garnish with diced bacon.

Fish and vegetable soup

(serves 4–5)

25 g butter
3 leeks, peeled and sliced
3 large potatoes, peeled and diced
2 c boiling water
salt and pepper
500 g cooked and flaked white fish
2 c milk
1 c frozen peas
2–3 T chopped chives or parsley (for garnish)

Melt butter in frying pan, add leeks, and fry gently until soft. Add potatoes, boiling water, salt and pepper. Cover and cook for 10 minutes. Add fish and simmer for a further 10 minutes. Add milk and peas, and simmer gently until heated. Adjust seasoning. Ladle into serving dishes and garnish with chives or parsley.

Cheese and onion soup

(serves 4–5)

2 T butter or oil
1 large onion, peeled and sliced
6 c beef stock (or water and stock cubes)
1 large potato, peeled and grated
1 c grated tasty cheese
2 T brandy (optional)
salt and pepper
soy sauce, Tabasco or Worcestershire sauce
parsley and croutons (for garnish)

Heat butter in a large saucepan, add onion and cook until golden brown. Add stock and bring to the boil. Add potato, reduce heat and allow to simmer for 15 minutes, or until the potato is cooked and the soup thickened. Add half the grated cheese and stir until it has melted. Remove from heat, add brandy, and adjust seasonings and sauces. Ladle into bowls, sprinkle extra cheese on top and garnish with parsley and croutons.

Caldo verde (Green soup)

(serves 4)

A soup from Portugal where kale and spinach are used. However, if substituting silverbeet, the soup will have a stronger flavour and deeper colour.

8 c hot water
1 t salt
4 large old potatoes, peeled and cut into chunks
500 g tender spinach or silverbeet
3 T olive oil
salt and freshly ground black pepper

In a saucepan, combine water, salt and potato chunks. Cook until soft. Remove potatoes and rub through a fine sieve. Leave the water in the saucepan. Wash spinach well, remove stalks and chop leaves very finely. Return sieved potato to the saucepan, add olive oil and spinach.

Cook over a high heat for 2–3 minutes, stirring well. Season to taste. Serve in large bowls with crusty bread.

Note: Soup can be blended in a food processor if a smoother texture is desired.

Minestrone soup

(serves 6–7)

1 c dried white beans (soaked overnight in 3 c water)
3 c beef stock (or water and stock cubes)
1 T cooking oil
1 large onion, peeled and chopped
2 medium potatoes, peeled and diced
1 clove garlic, peeled and chopped
2 large carrots, peeled and thinly sliced
2 stalks celery, chopped
$\frac{1}{2}$ c macaroni
salt and pepper
4 tomatoes, peeled and chopped
Parmesan cheese (for garnish)

Place beans and bean water in a large saucepan, add stock and simmer for 45–60 minutes. Heat cooking oil in frying pan, add onion, potatoes, garlic, carrots and celery. Sauté for 10 minutes. Add the vegetables to the beans and stock, cover, bring to boil, then simmer for 30 minutes, stirring occasionally. Add macaroni, salt, pepper and tomatoes. Simmer for 30 minutes until all vegetables are tender, adjust seasonings. Serve very hot in heated soup bowls. Serve Parmesan cheese separately.

Potato and avocado soup

(serves 5–6)

50 g butter
2 medium potatoes, peeled and diced
1 onion, peeled and chopped
1 clove garlic, peeled and crushed
2 ripe avocados, peeled, stoned and chopped
1 t curry powder
4 c chicken stock (or water and stock cubes)
salt and pepper
1 T lemon juice
croutons (for garnish)

Melt butter in saucepan, add potatoes, onion and garlic. Fry until onions are soft. Add avocado, curry powder and stock. Cover, bring to the boil, then reduce heat and simmer for 20 minutes. Purée or blend, reheat and season to taste. Add lemon juice. Serve garnished with croutons.

Note: To add a special touch, garnish with 1 t sour cream and three or four shrimps.

Mixed vegetable soup

(serves 4)

30 g butter
1 onion, peeled and sliced
1 large potato, peeled and chopped
1 small turnip, peeled and chopped
2 carrots, chopped
2 sticks celery, chopped
2 tomatoes, skinned and chopped
1 t paprika
salt and pepper
3 c stock (or water and stock cubes)
1 c milk
chopped chives

Heat butter in large saucepan, add onion and cook until golden brown. Add potato, turnip, carrots, celery and tomatoes. Sprinkle on paprika, salt and pepper, then add stock. Cover and simmer until all vegetables are tender. Purée or blend soup until smooth. Place milk in saucepan, then add the soup, heat (but do not boil). Adjust seasonings and pour into serving dishes. Sprinkle with chopped chives and serve.

Pumpkin and potato soup

(serves 4–6)

700–900 g pumpkin, peeled and chopped
1 large onion, peeled and chopped
2 medium potatoes, peeled and chopped
3 chicken stock cubes
8 c water
1 c natural yoghurt
salt and pepper
chopped chives (for garnish)

In a large saucepan, combine pumpkin, onion, potatoes, stock cubes and water. Bring to the boil, reduce heat and simmer uncovered for 20–25 minutes or until all vegetables are tender. Purée or blend until smooth. Bring back to the boil, stirring all the time. Add yoghurt, adjust seasoning and spoon into serving bowls. Top with chopped chives.

Note: Do not allow soup to boil after adding yoghurt. If too thick, dilute with a little water.

Microwaved bacon and cabbage soup

(makes 10–12 cups)

500 g lean bacon, diced
8 c hot water
1 large carrot, peeled and finely sliced
2 medium onions, peeled and chopped
1 parsnip, peeled and chopped
1 leek, finely sliced
1–2 t curry powder
4 medium potatoes, peeled and diced
500 g cabbage, finely shredded
salt and pepper

Place bacon and water in a large microproof bowl. Cover and cook on high power (100%) for 20 minutes. Skim off fat if necessary. Add all vegetables, except potatoes and cabbage, and the curry powder. Cook on high power for 15 minutes, then reduce to medium (50%) and cook a further 15 minutes. Add potatoes and cabbage, cook on high power till tender; about 12 minutes. Adjust seasoning. Serve with fresh brown bread or rolls.

Note: If cooking on the stove, allow 1–1½ hours, and add the potatoes and cabbage 20–30 minutes before the end of cooking time.

Microwaved potato and herb soup

(serves 4–5)

4 medium potatoes, peeled and diced
1 t salt
4 T water
2 T butter or margarine
1 onion, peeled and finely sliced into rings
1 T chopped fresh chervil
2 T freshly chopped parsley
2 T chopped chives
1 T paprika
5 c chicken stock (or water and chicken stock cubes)

Place potatoes in a large microproof bowl, dissolve salt in water and add to the potatoes. Cover and micro-cook on high power for 12 minutes or until tender, stirring once during the cooking time. Drain and mash the potatoes, then rub through a sieve, back into the bowl. In a small microproof bowl or jug, combine butter and onion, cook on high power for

2–3 minutes until tender. Mix the onion with potatoes, add herbs and paprika, and gradually stir in the chicken stock. Cover and micro-cook on high power for 15 minutes or until boiling. Reduce to medium power (50%) and cook a further 5 minutes. Season to taste, then stir and serve.

Fish chowder

(serves 3–4)

**400–500 g terakihi or similar
3 c water
1 onion, peeled and chopped
2 c milk
2–3 potatoes, peeled and chopped
1–2 t salt
pepper to taste
1–2 t butter
chopped parsley or chives (for garnish)**

Place the fish, water and onion in a large saucepan. Cover and cook for 20 minutes. Strain off liquid, remove and discard any bones and skin. Flake fish and set aside. Return the strained stock to the saucepan, add the milk, potatoes, salt and pepper to taste. Simmer gently until potatoes are soft. Add fish and stir in butter. Serve sprinkled with parsley or chives.

Note: A few drops of chilli or red pepper sauce give this dish a subtle tang. If a smoother texture is required, blend in a food processor.

Salads

Red and green potato salad

(serves 4–6)

Fresh herbs give flavour to this salad.

6 medium potatoes
6–8 bacon rashers
1 red onion, peeled and chopped
$\frac{1}{4}$ c white vinegar
$\frac{1}{4}$ c olive oil
2 t dry mustard
salt and pepper
2 T chopped fresh tarragon
1 c fresh chopped parsley

Scrub or peel the potatoes and cut into small cubes. Cook in salted water until tender but not soft or broken. Drain and keep warm.

Fry the bacon until crisp, remove rind and chop into small pieces. Put aside. Add onion to hot bacon fat and cook until soft. Remove from the heat and whisk in vinegar, oil, mustard, salt and pepper. Place the potatoes in a serving bowl and pour the bacon dressing over them. Add tarragon and parsley, toss gently to combine. Add bacon and serve.

Confetti potato salad

(serves 4–6)

Small red potatoes give extra colour to this salad, but you can substitute any small new potatoes that do not require peeling. The ingredients and quantities can be varied — these are a guide only.

1 kg small new red potatoes
1 medium carrot
4–5 spring onions
3–4 hardboiled eggs, shelled and sliced
2 T chopped fresh dill
2 T chopped fresh parsley
$^1\!/_2$ t salt
$^1\!/_2$ t freshly ground black pepper
$^1\!/_2$ c sour cream
1 c mayonnaise

Scrub the potatoes and cut in half. Cook until just tender in boiling salted water. Drain and cool. Grate the carrot and chop the spring onions. Place these in a serving bowl with potatoes and eggs. Add dill, parsley, salt and pepper, gently toss to combine. Mix the sour cream and mayonnaise, and gently fold into the mixture. Cover and refrigerate for 2–4 hours.

Fish and potato salad

(serves 4)

1 c sour cream
2 T prepared horseradish sauce
1 small onion, peeled and chopped
1 t lemon juice
salt and pepper
1 T dried dill
500 g any cooked fish, boned and cubed
4 medium potatoes, cooked and cubed
2 hardboiled eggs
parsley
slices of tomato

In a bowl combine sour cream, horseradish sauce, onion, lemon juice, salt, pepper and dill. Beat well. Carefully fold in the cooked fish and potato. Cover and refrigerate for at least 30 minutes. Stir carefully again and place on a salad dish. Slice eggs, and arrange on top of the salad with the parsley and tomato.

German potato salad

(serves 4–6)

6 medium potatoes
1 medium onion, peeled and chopped
½ c chicken stock
3 T olive oil
1 T wholegrain seed mustard
1 T wine vinegar
1 t salt
½ t pepper
1 T lemon juice

Peel and cut potatoes into chunks, and boil in salted water until just tender. Drain and keep warm. In a saucepan, combine onion, chicken stock, olive oil, mustard, wine vinegar, salt and pepper. Simmer for 5–6 minutes, stir in lemon juice. Pour this dressing over the warm potatoes. Stir once or twice before serving.

Hot kumara salad

(serves 3–4)

3–4 kumara, cooked and cut into chunks
1 red onion, peeled and thinly sliced
1 c cooked, chopped green beans
2–4 gherkins, sliced
3 rashers bacon, cooked until crisp
½–1 c sour cream
½–1 t dry mustard

Preheat oven to 180°C. Place kumara, onion, beans and gherkins in an ovenproof dish. Add crumbled bacon. Combine sour cream and mustard, and stir gently into vegetables. Bake for 15–20 minutes or until kumara is thoroughly heated.

Note: Take care not to boil the sour cream. This salad can also be served cold.

Indian potato salad

(serves 3–4)

1 T tamarind, dried pulp
$^1/_4$ c hot water
2–3 medium potatoes
1 small onion, peeled and finely chopped
1–2 fresh green chillies, seeded and finely chopped
$^1/_2$ t salt
$^1/_2$ t chilli powder
1 T fresh coriander leaves, chopped

Soak the tamarind in the hot water for 20 minutes. Squeeze out and reserve the liquid. Scrub or peel potatoes, cut into medium slices and cook in boiling water until just tender. Drain and cool. Combine tamarind liquid, potatoes, onion and all other ingredients. Mix gently. Serve cold.

Spicy potato salad

(serves 3–4)

This easy-to-prepare salad is better made early in the day so the flavours have time to mix. If a red onion is not available, substitute an ordinary one.

500 g cooked, thinly sliced potatoes
1 medium red onion, peeled and sliced into rings
1 t salt
1 t freshly ground black pepper
1–2 T chopped chives
4 T olive oil
3 T white wine vinegar

Arrange potato slices and onion rings in alternate layers in a shallow dish. Sprinkle with salt, pepper and chives. Combine the oil and vinegar in a screwtop jar and shake well. Pour this dressing over the potatoes and onions. Cover the dish and refrigerate for 6–8 hours before serving.

Yoghurt and potato salad

(serves 4–5)

2 c natural yoghurt
500 g boiled potatoes, cubed
1 small onion, peeled and chopped
salt and pepper
1 green chilli, seeded and finely chopped
$\frac{1}{2}$ red pepper, seeded and finely sliced
$\frac{1}{2}$ t ground cumin
1 T chopped coriander leaves

Beat the yoghurt in a bowl until smooth. Gently fold in potatoes, onion, salt, pepper, chilli, red pepper and cumin. Serve sprinkled with chopped coriander.

Sour cream potato salad

(serves 4–5)

Cold roast beef, ham, salami, drained tinned tuna or salmon can be used.

1 c chopped cold meat or fish
2 large potatoes, cooked and cubed
1 large beetroot, cooked, peeled and cubed
1 large cooking apple, peeled, cored and cubed
1 cucumber, peeled and cubed
200 ml sour cream
1 T vinegar
1 t dry mustard
parsley, watercress, tomatoes, fresh herbs (for garnish)

Combine meat, potatoes, beetroot, apple and cucumber. Mix together sour cream, vinegar and mustard, and stir into meat and vegetables. Pack into a small ring mould and leave in the refrigerator until just before serving. Turn the mould out onto a serving dish. Arrange parsley, watercress, slices of tomatoes or fresh herbs in the middle.

Extra spicy potato salad

(serves 6–8)

You can adjust the spices if you wish, but be careful — no one flavour should dominate.

6 large potatoes, peeled and diced
2 T vegetable oil
1 t mustard powder
2 tomatoes, peeled and diced
1/2 green pepper, seeded and diced
1/4 t cayenne pepper
1/4 t ground turmeric
1/4 t ground allspice
1 t ground ginger
1/2 t salt
1 t sugar
1/4 t ground coriander

Cook potatoes in boiling water until tender, drain immediately, then replace lid on the saucepan to keep the potatoes hot. In a large frying pan, heat the vegetable oil, add all the other ingredients and cook until bubbling, stirring constantly. Carefully stir the potatoes into the mixture until they are hot and well coated with the spices. Serve immediately.

Potato salad with horseradish dressing

(serves 4)

1 kg new baby potatoes, scrubbed
1/2 c sour cream
2–3 T finely grated horseradish
1 t honey
salt and pepper
chopped parsley and chives (for garnish)

Boil new potatoes until just tender and slice each in half. Keep warm. Combine sour cream, horseradish, honey, salt and pepper and stir into the potatoes until they are well coated. Sprinkle with parsley and chives. Serve warm or chilled.

Note: Prepared horseradish is now available. Adjust the quantity according to taste. For an extra quick salad, spoon 1 c of horseradish mayonnaise over the warm potatoes and then sprinkle on the parsley and chives.

Salmon salad

(serves 4–6)

1 kg potatoes, cooked and diced
$^1/_4$–$^1/_2$ c mayonnaise
$^1/_2$–1 c drained salmon or tuna, flaked
3–4 gherkins, finely chopped
1–2 hard boiled eggs, shelled and chopped
salt and pepper
chopped parsley

Cool potatoes. Combine mayonnaise, salmon, gherkins, eggs, salt and pepper and stir into potatoes. Sprinkle with parsley.

Note: For extra tang, add a few drops of Tabasco sauce to the mayonnaise.

Potatoes plus

Baked stuffed potatoes/sweet potatoes/kumara

Wash or scrub the skins and bake or microwave until soft to touch (turn part way through cooking as some will cook more quickly than others). Cut the cooked potato in half lengthwise. Scoop out the flesh, leaving a thick wall of potato and skin. Mix the flesh with any of the following (vary quantities to suit individual tastes):

Fillings

Sour cream, cracked pepper, shallots or chives.
Chopped mushrooms and bacon.
Grated cheese and pickle.
Smoked fish and parsley or chopped onion.
Grated tasty cheese, beaten egg and parsley.
Grated cheese, sardines and tomato paste.
Cooked diced chicken and mayonnaise.
Cooked chopped vegetables and mayonnaise.
Baked beans, chilli sauce, sour cream and cheese.
Egg yolk, cheese and chives.
Cooked chopped meat and pickle.
Fresh herbs and cheese.
Blue vein cheese, tomato sauce and fresh basil.
Chopped ham, mustard and tasty cheese.

Toppings

Bake or microwave potatoes, cut a cross in the top to expose some of the flesh, then spoon over one of these toppings and serve.

Sour cream or cottage cheese with chives or parsley.
Crushed garlic and melted butter.
Fried onion with tomato, mushroom or bacon.

Grated cheese and fresh herbs.
Blue cheese, cream and tomato sauce.
Melted butter and parsley

Stuffings

The flesh from baked potatoes can be combined with fruit and vegetables
and used as a base for stuffings.

Chicken stuffing: cooked potato flesh, chopped onion, egg, thyme, butter
and seasoning. Also any of these can be added for extra flavour —
mushrooms, chopped bacon, celery, whole kernel corn.

Fruit stuffing (for chicken or meat): cooked potato flesh, chopped onion, 6-
8 dried chopped apricots, 1/4 c sultanas, 1 large apple, peeled and
chopped, salt and pepper, dried mixed herbs, prunes or crushed drained
pineapple.

Potato chips

Mention the words "potato chips" and, depending on the age of the person,
each may have a different idea of what you mean. Peeling and making
chips, and cautions on the dangers of hot fat, were often among the first
lessons learned in the school home economics courses.

Packets of potato chips or crisps appeared in New Zealand in the early
1960s. They can be served with a meal, a salad, or on their own with dips.
Also try different seasonings with the chips, or provide small labelled
containers so that your guests can experiment.

Different ways of cutting the potato, along with the size and the thickness
of the slices, will often denote a different name. Names of chips often refer
to the shape in which they are cut before deep frying; for example,
matchsticks, straw, game chips and wafer. French fries are chips sliced
into thin strips and deep fried in cooking oil. Chips are generally thicker, and
were originally deep fried in animal fat (suet). It is more common now for all
types to be deep fried in cooking oil.

Potato skins have become very popular in the last five years, and are now
served as entrées or with pre-dinner drinks.

Saratoga chips

Wash and peel potatoes, then slice very thinly (the slices should be nearly
transparent when held up to the light). Place in cold water for at least 1 hour,
then drain and dry thoroughly. Heat oil until smoking, add chips and cook
until crisp and brown. Drain well, sprinkle with salt and serve.

Variations: Sprinkle the cooked chips or crisps with Parmesan cheese, freshly mixed herbs, Italian herbs, curry powder, or rock salt and freshly ground pepper.

Note: Take care that the chips are dry before adding to the hot oil or it will splatter. Cook a few at a time so the temperature of the oil does not drop.

Pommes Parisienne (Fried potato balls)

(makes 15–20)

A classic French recipe.

**3–4 large old potatoes
butter**

Peel potatoes and place in cold water to stop discoloration. Using a melon ball cutter, scoop out the potatoes into small balls. (Reserve any trimmings and outer surface for soup, or use for mashed potato.)

Blanch or parboil the small potato balls in boiling water. Drain well. Heat the butter and sauté the potato balls until golden brown. Drain on paper towels. Serve with salads and cold meats.

Sweet potato with orange glaze

(serves 4)

**4 medium sweet potatoes
$^1/_2$ c orange juice
2 T brown sugar
1 T arrowroot (or cornflour)
$^1/_2$ c water
grated orange rind (for garnish)
chopped spring onions or chives (for garnish)**

Cut sweet potatoes into 2.5-mm thick slices, and cook in salted boiling water until just tender; about 10–15 minutes. Drain and keep warm. In a small saucepan, combine orange juice, sugar, arrowroot and water. Stir well. Heat gently until the sauce has thickened, stirring constantly. Arrange sweet potato on a serving plate, spoon over the glaze and sprinkle with orange rind and chopped spring onions or chives.

Duchess potatoes

(makes 6–8)

4 medium sized potatoes, peeled and chopped
boiling salted water
1 egg, separated
1 T butter
salt and pepper
2 T water

Preheat oven to 230°C. Cook potatoes in boiling water until soft. Drain. Sieve, then add egg yolk, butter and seasoning. Beat well and spoon into a piping bag with a large star nozzle. Pipe the mixture in neat spirals onto a greased oven tray. Beat egg white with water until fluffy. Place potatoes in hot oven for 3–4 minutes to set the edges, then remove from the oven and brush egg white over potato mixture. Return to oven until lightly brown.

Potatoes in cream

(serves 3–4)

4 medium sized potatoes, scrubbed and quartered
milk
salt and pepper
2 T cream
freshly chopped parsley (for garnish)

Boil potatoes in their skins until soft, drain and cool slightly. Peel and cut into slices. Place in a frying pan and add enough milk to just cover the potatoes. (The amount will depend on the size of the potatoes and the depth of the frying pan). Season well. Allow to simmer for 10 minutes then add cream, toss gently, and sprinkle with parsley.

Spicy potato balls

(makes 20)

These take a little time to prepare, and are ideally served with a green salad. The different spices are important, even when used in small quantities.

2 T oil
1 large onion, peeled and finely chopped
2 cloves garlic, peeled and chopped
2 cm root ginger, grated
1 t ground turmeric
$^1/_4$ t chilli powder
1 t salt
1 T vinegar
500 g minced lamb
1 t garam marsala
1 kg potatoes, peeled and boiled
1 t salt
1 t cumin seed
milk to mix if required
1 egg, beaten with 2 T water
dried breadcrumbs
oil for shallow frying

Heat oil in a heavy-based frying pan. Add onion, garlic and ginger, and fry for 4–5 minutes until golden brown. Add turmeric, chilli powder, salt and vinegar, stir well, then add the minced lamb. Cover, lower heat and cook for 20 minutes, stirring occasionally.

Remove cover, increase heat, stir constantly and cook until the liquid has evaporated and the lamb is dry. Mix in the garam marsala and leave to cool. Mash potatoes with salt, cumin seed and milk. Divide into 20 balls. (Wet fingers to make the potato easier to mould.) Take a ball of potato (about the size of a golf ball) and make a depression in the middle. Fill this with the cool meat mixture and reform the potato, making sure that no cracks appear. Prepare others in the same way. Dip in egg and breadcrumbs.

Heat oil over a high heat and fry the potato balls until golden brown, turning constantly to ensure an even colour. Drain on paper towels and then serve.

Sliced potato cake

(serves 4–6)

4–5 large old potatoes, peeled and thinly sliced
salt and pepper
100 g melted butter

Preheat oven to 200°C. Wash and dry potatoes thoroughly.

Butter a shallow ovenproof dish or non-stick cake tin, and cover the base with overlapping potato slices. Sprinkle with salt and pepper, and brush with melted butter. Continue with layers of potato, salt and pepper and melted butter until all the potato is used. Cover the dish and bake for 45–60 minutes. Stand for 5 minutes, then run a knife around the potatoes to unmould. Turn out onto a heated plate, cut into wedges.

Pommes Dauphine (Cream puff potatoes)

(makes 15–20)

Pommes Dauphine (a classic French recipe) are made from equal quantities of choux pastry and mashed potato. The pastry can be made a few days in advance and kept in the refrigerator. They are best served soon after frying, as they soften if kept warm for too long.

Choux pastry

3 T butter
1/2 c water
1/2 c flour
2 eggs

250 g cold mashed potato
oil for frying

In a saucepan, bring butter and water to the boil. Sift in the flour and stir until the mixture leaves the side of the saucepan. Allow the mixture to cool. Beat in the eggs until the mixture is smooth and has a shiny appearance.

Add the mashed potato to the choux pastry, beat well until blended. Place in large teaspoonfuls on a cold tray or, using a piping bag, pipe shapes or crowns. Heat oil in a deep pan and gradually add spoonfuls of mixture. Cook for 5–6 minutes until puffs are well risen and golden brown. Serve immediately.

Note: To keep the oil hot and at an even temperature, do not add too much mixture at once.

Cheese and bacon potatoes

(serves 4)

3–4 bacon rashers
1 T oil or butter
1–2 medium onions, peeled and sliced
3–4 large potatoes, peeled and sliced
1 c chicken stock (or water and stock cubes)
salt and pepper
½–1 c grated tasty cheese

Preheat oven to 190°C. Remove rind and chop bacon into small pieces. Melt oil or butter in a frying pan, add the bacon and fry until crisp. Remove bacon and fry the sliced onion in the remaining fat. Take care not to brown the onion. Transfer bacon and onion to an ovenproof dish, add sliced potatoes, pour over stock, add salt and pepper as required. Sprinkle grated cheese on top and bake uncovered for 45–60 minutes or until the potatoes are tender.

Pommes gratinées (potato and cheese)

(serves 2–3)

Another classic French recipe, this is best if the potatoes are still warm after being sieved and mixed, then placed under the grill.

3–4 large potatoes, cooked and sieved
1 T butter
salt and pepper
1 c grated tasty cheese
2–3 T dried breadcrumbs

Preheat grill. Combine the potato, butter, salt and pepper until smooth. Spoon into a greased ovenproof dish. Sprinkle the cheese on top, then cover lightly with the breadcrumbs. Place under the grill until the cheese is golden brown, and serve immediately.

Opposite: Kumara and orange soup, page 12. (Photograph and recipe courtesy of the New Zealand Vegetable Growers' Federation.)

Gnocchi with tomato sauce

(serves 2–3)

300 g potato, mashed and sieved
1/2 c flour
1 egg, beaten
25 g butter
salt, pepper, grated nutmeg

Tomato sauce

1 T butter
1 onion, peeled and chopped
2 stalks celery, chopped
1 T flour
2 T tomato paste
4 tomatoes, skinned and chopped
1 c water
1 t mixed herbs
salt and pepper

Combine potato, flour, beaten egg, butter and seasonings. Mould into walnut-sized balls. Dust well with flour and flatten slightly with a fork. Simmer in water for 5 minutes, drain carefully and place in greased casserole dish. Cover with prepared tomato sauce, sprinkle with grated cheese and brown lightly under a hot grill.

Tomato sauce: Melt butter and sauté onion and celery until tender. Stir in flour, brown lightly, then stir in tomato paste, tomatoes, water, herbs, salt and pepper. Bring to the boil and simmer gently uncovered for 30 minutes. Purée or blend until smooth.

Sautéed potatoes with breadcrumbs

(serves 4)

1 kg old potatoes, freshly boiled in their skins
100 g ghee or clarified butter
1/2–1 c fresh breadcrumbs
salt and freshly ground black pepper

Skin the potatoes and cut into chunks. Heat a heavy-based frying pan, add ghee and, when foaming, add the potatoes. Allow the potatoes to colour slightly before turning, then turn frequently until all sides are golden brown. Add breadcrumbs and cook until they are crisp and brown. Add seasonings. Serve immediately.

Opposite: Kumara split, page 39. (Photograph and recipe courtesy of the New Zealand Vegetable Growers' Federation.)

Vegetable curry

(serves 4–5)

Although this recipe has a large number of ingredients, any other vegetables can be used as well, 1–2 T of curry powder can be used as a substitute for the spices, though the flavour will not be quite the same. This dish can be served hot or cold.

2 T oil
2 onions, peeled and sliced
1 clove garlic, peeled and chopped
1 apple, peeled, cored and chopped
2.5 cm fresh root ginger, peeled and chopped
1 T mustard seeds
1 t turmeric
1 t coriander seeds
1 t ground cumin
$^1/_2$ t ground fenugreek
$^1/_2$ t chilli powder
2 c chicken stock (or water and stock cubes)
grated rind and juice of 1/2 lemon
freshly ground black pepper
3 c peeled and cubed potatoes
1 c peeled and sliced carrots
3 tomatoes, peeled and chopped
2 c cauliflower florets
1 c sliced green beans (or peas)
$^1/_2$ c sultanas or raisins
1–2 T grated fresh coconut

Heat oil in a large frying pan or saucepan. Add onions, garlic, apple and ginger, fry gently for 5 minutes, stirring occasionally. Stir in the spices, cook for 3–4 minutes. Add stock and bring to boil, stirring constantly. Add lemon rind, juice and pepper to taste. Add potatoes, carrots and tomatoes, cover and simmer for 10 minutes. Add cauliflower, beans and sultanas, cover and simmer for a further 10 minutes, until the vegetables are tender but not broken up. Adjust the seasoning and sprinkle with coconut.

Note: Apart from using other vegetables, $^1/_2$–1 c of shelled brazil nuts or walnuts can be added with the second lot of vegetables. Dried shredded coconut soaked in milk for 15 minutes can replace the fresh coconut.

Sweet potato and apple casserole

(serves 4–5)

4 medium sweet potatoes, peeled and thinly sliced
4 medium cooking apples, cored, peeled and sliced
1 t salt
$^1\!/_2$ c brown sugar
1 t cinnamon
75 g butter
$^1\!/_2$ c raisins
2 T lemon juice
4 T water

Preheat oven to 180°C. Layer sweet potatoes and apple slices into a greased casserole dish, sprinkling each layer with salt, sugar, cinnamon, small chunks of butter, and raisins. Pour the liquid and any remaining butter over the mixture. Cover the casserole and bake for 40–60 minutes or until the vegetables are soft. Serve as a vegetable casserole or with roast meat.

Tortilla (Spanish potato omelette)

(serves 3–4)

1 T butter
1 T oil
2 bacon rashers
1 large onion, peeled and thinly sliced
2 medium potatoes, boiled, peeled and sliced
$^1\!/_2$ t salt
freshly ground black pepper to taste
4 eggs, lightly beaten

Heat butter and oil in a frying pan. Add bacon and cook until crisp, remove from pan. In the remaining fat, fry the onion until soft. Spread the potato slices over the onion, add seasoning. Cut bacon into small pieces and sprinkle over potato. Pour eggs over vegetables and cook until the omelette has started to set around the edges.

Lift the cooked edges with a spatula and tilt the frying pan so that the uncooked egg flows underneath. Repeat until no uncooked egg is left, but the centre is still moist. Invert the omelette on to a large plate, then slide it back into the pan, cooked side up. Continue cooking over a low heat for 2–3 minutes until the omelette is set and firm. Cut into wedges and serve hot or cold.

Potato cheese dumplings with tomato herb sauce

(serves 4)

Dumplings

4 medium potatoes, peeled, diced, cooked, and kept warm
50 g butter
1–2 T milk
½ c flour
1 t crushed garlic
2 c grated tasty cheese
2 eggs
salt and pepper to taste

Tomato herb sauce

1 T oil
1 onion, peeled and chopped
6–8 medium-sized tomatoes, peeled and chopped
¼ c white wine
2 T chopped parsley
¼ c chopped fresh basil
1 T sugar
salt and pepper

Mash the potatoes with butter and milk until smooth. Add sifted flour, garlic, cheese, eggs, salt and pepper. Mix well and allow to cool. Using lightly floured hands, roll the potato mixture into balls about the size of a table tennis ball. Drop these dumplings into boiling water and cook until they rise to the top of the water. (Only cook 4–6 at once, depending on the size of the saucepan.) Remove from water using a slotted spoon and keep warm while cooking the rest.

To serve, arrange dumplings on a dish and pour over the tomato herb sauce. Sprinkle with Parmesan cheese if desired.

Sauce: Heat oil in frying pan, add chopped onion and sauté until tender. Add tomatoes and white wine, bring to the boil and simmer for 5 minutes. Add parsley, basil, sugar, salt and pepper. Cook for 1–2 minutes then pour over the dumplings.

Hash browns

(serves 2–3)

Hash browns are a popular American breakfast dish, although now often served with grilled meats as part of a light evening meal.

3–4 medium potatoes, peeled and sliced
2 T cooking oil
1 T butter
salt and pepper

Parboil potatoes in salted water for 7–10 minutes. Drain. Heat cooking oil and butter in a large frying pan, add potato slices, sprinkle with salt and pepper and fry until browned. Serve immediately.

Note: The cooked and seasoned potatoes can be mashed, then browned in the hot butter and oil. A small peeled and minced onion added to the cooked potato gives extra flavour to the dish. For a milder flavour, cook the onion in the oil before adding potato.

Candied sweet potatoes

(serves 4)

4–5 medium sweet potatoes, peeled and thickly sliced
salt and pepper
1 T grated orange zest
juice of 1 large orange
$1/2$ c brown sugar
1 t ground cinnamon
1 T grated fresh ginger (or less if preferred)
2 T butter

Preheat oven to 200°C. Parboil potatoes until just tender. Arrange on the base of a large flat casserole or pie dish, overlapping but not completely covering another slice. Sprinkle with salt and pepper and orange rind, and pour over orange juice. Add sugar, cinnamon and ginger. Place small amounts of butter on top. Bake uncovered for 30 minutes or until the topping is bubbling, basting occasionally. Serve immediately.

Bacon and potato savoury

(serves 4–5)

4–6 bacon rashers
4 medium potatoes, peeled
2 cloves garlic, peeled and crushed
300 ml sour cream
3 eggs, beaten
1 medium onion, peeled and chopped
2 T freshly chopped parsley
1 c grated tasty cheese
salt and pepper

Grill bacon until crisp, then chop into squares. Preheat oven to 200°C. Grate potatoes and squeeze well to remove excess water. Drain on paper towel. In a bowl combine garlic, sour cream and eggs, mix until smooth. Add potatoes, onion, bacon, parsley, cheese, salt and pepper. Spoon into a shallow greased ovenware dish and bake for 30–40 minutes, or until crisp and golden brown. Serve with a fresh green salad.

Potato balls

(makes 6)

2 c cooked mashed potato
2 t onion stock
2 t Parmesan cheese
flour
beaten egg
breadcrumbs
oil

Combine potato, stock and cheese, and roll into balls about the size of a golf ball. Roll in flour, then beaten egg, and lastly breadcrumbs. Refrigerate for at least 30 minutes. Preheat oil in a frying pan and cook potato balls until golden brown. Serve with a salad or cold meat and pickle.

Kumara split

(serves 4)

4 medium kumara/sweet potato (approx 1 kg)

Scrub the kumara/sweet potato and bake at 180°C for 45–55 minutes, or until soft. Cut in half lengthwise and fill with one of the following fillings. Return to the oven for 5–10 minutes or until the filling is well heated.

Fillings

Mushroom. Combine 2 c finely chopped mushrooms, $^1/_2$ c low fat sour cream, 2 T chives, freshly ground black pepper, 1 t toasted sesame seeds.

Mediterranean. Combine 1 onion, finely chopped, 4 tomatoes, roughly chopped, $^1/_4$ c low fat sour cream, $^1/_2$ t dried basil or 1 T finely chopped fresh basil, 3 T grated Parmesan cheese.

Mussel. Combine 2 c finely chopped mussels, $^1/_3$ c coconut cream, 4 spring onions, finely sliced.

Potato and cheese puffs

(makes 8–12)

2–3 c cold mashed potato
2 eggs, separated
grated cheese
salt and pepper

Preheat oven to 180°C. Combine potato with egg yolks, cheese, salt and pepper. Beat egg whites until stiff and fold into potato mixture. Using 2 dessertspoons, drop the portions of the mixture onto a greased oven tray. Bake for 15–20 minutes until set and golden brown.

Caraway potatoes

(serves 4)

Potatoes cooked this way retain a distinctive caraway seed flavour.

500 g small new potatoes, scrubbed and pricked
$^1/_2$ c melted butter
1 t sugar
1 T caraway seeds
$^1/_2$ t salt

Place all ingredients in a medium-sized saucepan, cover and cook over a very low heat for 30–35 minutes. Shake the saucepan frequently as no water is added. Potatoes are cooked when easily pierced with a sharp knife. Turn out onto a heated dish and serve.

Microwaved baked kumara

(serves 4)

4 medium kumara
2 T butter, melted, or cooking oil
sour cream and chives for garnish

Scrub the kumara. Choose vegetables of similar size to ensure even cooking. Prick the skins, brush with butter or oil. (This stops the skin from drying out and becoming tough.) Place on a large plate and micro-cook on high power (100%) for 15–18 minutes, turning the kumara every 5 minutes, until they feel soft when pierced with a toothpick. Slit across the top, garnish with sour cream and chives.

Crispy potato cakes

(serves 4–6)

3 large old potatoes
2 eggs
1 small onion, peeled and chopped
1 T flour
salt and pepper
4 T oil

Peel potatoes and grate into a bowl of cold water. Drain, and squeeze well to remove excess moisture. Dry with paper towel. Beat eggs and add to the grated potato with onion, flour, salt and pepper. Heat oil in a large frying pan. Spoon a large tablespoon of potato mixture into the hot oil. Spread it out well. (This makes for quicker cooking and a crisper cake.) When golden brown underneath, turn over and cook the other side until brown. Drain on paper towel and keep warm until the rest of the cakes have been cooked. Serve with a poached egg or mixed grill.

Potatoes with sour cream

(serves 3–4)

3–4 potatoes, peeled and diced
2 T butter
salt and pepper
1–2 T chopped chives
$^{1}/_{2}$–1 c sour cream

Cook the diced potatoes in boiling salted water until just tender. Drain. Melt butter in a frying pan, brown the potatoes, then add salt and pepper. Add chopped chives and sour cream. Cover and simmer over a low heat until all the cream is absorbed. Serve hot with cold meat or fish dishes.

Kumara and orange bake

(serves 3–4)

3–4 large kumara, peeled, cooked and mashed
grated rind and juice of 1 orange
salt and pepper
1 c finely crushed potato chips
25 g butter

Preheat oven to 180°C. Mix together mashed kumara, orange rind and juice, salt and pepper. Place in a greased ovenproof dish. Top with potato chips and dot with butter. Bake for about 15 minutes or until brown. Serve with any meat and a green salad.

Mock whitebait fritters

(makes 4–6)

1 egg
2 T flour
2 T milk
$^{1}/_{2}$ t salt
freshly ground black pepper
1 medium potato, peeled and grated
1 t baking powder
oil for frying

Preheat frying pan. Beat egg, then add flour, milk, salt and pepper. Stir in potato and baking powder. Drop dessertspoonfuls into hot fat, fry until brown, turn and fry the other side. Drain on paper towels, then serve.

Potato and carrot mould

(serves 4–5)

3 medium potatoes, peeled and chopped
3 carrots, peeled and chopped
1 c warm milk
1 egg, beaten
salt and pepper
2 T butter
$\frac{1}{2}$ t ground nutmeg

Preheat oven to 180°C. Cook potatoes and carrots in boiling salted water until tender. Drain, and mash with milk, egg, salt and pepper, butter and nutmeg. Beat until fluffy. Pour into a greased ring mould and bake for 20 minutes or until browned and set. Serve with green vegetables, roast beef and horseradish sauce.

Sweet potato-pineapple kebabs

(serves 4–5)

4 medium kumara/sweet potatoes, cooked and cut into cubes
250 g canned or fresh pineapple pieces
4 apples, quartered and cored
2 red or green peppers, seeded, cut in chunks
75–100 g melted butter
3 t cinnamon
$\frac{1}{2}$ t ground cloves
$\frac{1}{2}$ t ground nutmeg
3 T lemon juice

Preheat grill. Thread onto a skewer kumara chunks alternated with pineapple pieces, apple and peppers. Combine butter, cinnamon, cloves, nutmeg and lemon juice, and brush thickly over the kebabs. Grill, turning and basting frequently until lightly browned. Serve with pork or chicken, and salads.

Potato savouries

(makes 12)

12 slices bread, buttered and crusts removed
2 c cooked mashed potato
1 onion, peeled and finely chopped
$\frac{1}{2}$–1 c tuna, drained and flaked
1 egg, beaten
$\frac{1}{2}$ c grated tasty cheese
1 t chilli sauce
salt and pepper
chopped chives or parsley
butter

Preheat oven to 160°C. Line patty pans with buttered bread, face down. Combine all ingredients, except butter, and spoon into bread cases. Place a dot of butter on the top of each savoury. Bake for 30 minutes or until crisp and brown. Serve hot or cold.

Potato fritters

(makes 12–14)

Batter

1 c flour
$\frac{1}{2}$ t baking powder
2 T oil
$\frac{1}{2}$ c water
1 egg white

3–4 medium potatoes, peeled
oil for deep frying

To make batter, sift flour and baking powder, stir in oil and water, beat well and stand for at least 30 minutes. Cut potatoes into approximately 6-mm slices, place in boiling salted water and boil for 1–2 minutes. Drain, rinse under cold water, then pat each slice dry.

Preheat oil for deep frying. Beat egg white until very stiff and stir lightly into the prepared batter. Dip each potato slice into batter and deep fry until golden brown and crisp. Drain on paper towel, sprinkle with salt if desired before serving.

Note: Sweet potato (kumara) can be cooked in the same way. Do not add too many potato slices to the hot oil at once, as this will cause the temperature to drop and the slices will not brown as quickly.

Potato pumpkin cakes

(makes 4–5)

1 large potato, peeled and grated
1 piece of pumpkin (same size as potato), peeled and seeded
1 small onion, peeled
1 clove garlic, peeled and crushed
freshly ground black pepper
1 egg, beaten
1 T light soy sauce
1 T chopped parsley
oil

Soak potato in cold water for 10 minutes, then drain and squeeze well to remove excess moisture. Grate pumpkin and onion, then mix with potato. Add garlic, pepper, egg, soy sauce and parsley. Shape into 4–5 cakes. Heat oil in frying pan, add cakes, pressing to flatten. Cook until golden brown and set, turn and brown other side. Serve hot as a vegetable dish.

Two-potato bake

(serves 6–8)

8 large old potatoes
2 c cooked mashed sweet potato/kumara
salt and pepper
2–3 T hot milk
$\frac{1}{4}$ c crushed drained pineapple
few drops Tabasco sauce
melted butter
grated cheese

Preheat oven to 180°C. Scrub and bake potatoes until soft when pierced with a toothpick; about 40–60 minutes. Remove from oven and cut a 2-cm slice lengthwise from each. Scoop out the centres of the potatoes and mash. Combine sweet potato, salt and pepper, milk, pineapple, Tabasco sauce and 1 c mashed potato. Mix well to make a smooth piping consistency, adding melted butter or extra potato if required. Place mixture in a piping bag, and pipe into the potato shells. Sprinkle with cheese and grill until tops are golden brown. Serve immediately.

Scalloped potatoes

(serves 4)

3 medium potatoes, unpeeled and sliced
1 medium onion, sliced
$1/2$ c milk
freshly ground black pepper
1 t butter or margarine
$1/2$ c grated cheese (optional)

Layer potato slices and separated onion rings into an 8-cup capacity baking dish. Add milk. Season generously with pepper and dot with the butter. Sprinkle with cheese. Bake at 180°C for 40–45 minutes, or until tender and golden brown.

Chunky skins

(makes 12)

3 large potatoes
1 T oil
pinch of paprika

Wash the potatoes. Thickly peel the potato (about $3/4$–1 cm thick). Brush the peels with the oil and sprinkle with paprika. Bake at 200°C for 40–50 minutes, or until crunchy and golden brown. Serve either as a snack or with a main meal.

Note: Use the centre of the potato for the next day — just immerse in water until ready to use.

Microwaved Pukekohe nuggets

(serves 2–3)

Some people say this is the only way to eat freshly dug, new-season baby potatoes. Try it and decide for yourself.

450 g new baby potatoes
3 T butter
2 T water
2 sprigs of mint
2 T chopped mint (for garnish)

Scrub and prick the potatoes. Place in a ring mould with butter, water and sprigs of mint. Cover and micro-cook on high power (100%) for 8–10 minutes, stirring once during the cooking time. Drain if required, or just remove the cooked mint and sprinkle with freshly chopped mint. Do not overcook.

Microwaved potato surprise

(serves 4–6)

800 g potatoes, peeled and grated
1 medium onion, peeled and grated
3–4 slices bacon, trimmed and chopped into small pieces
1 c grated tasty cheese
2 T milk
1 t salt
pinch of nutmeg
sliced tomatoes, cooked peas, beans or baby carrots (for garnish)

Wash the grated potato to remove starch, then drain and squeeze well to remove excess water. Combine potato, onion, bacon, cheese, milk, salt and nutmeg. Press into a 20-cm micro-proof ring mould. (Potato will condense down when cooked.) Cover and micro-cook, elevated, on high power (100%) for 15–18 minutes, until potato is tender. Stand for 5 minutes, turn onto plate and garnish with tomatoes, peas, etc.

Note: Cooking time and texture will vary according to the type of potato used.

Microwaved (or baked) hassleback or fan potatoes

(serves 4–6)

6 medium potatoes
4 T butter, melted
2 t garlic stock powder
4 T dried breadcrumbs
4 T grated tasty cheese

Peel potatoes or scrub well. Make 1-cm wide cuts across the potatoes, but do not cut completely through. Place the potatoes in cold water for 10 minutes to remove excess starch. Drain and dry. Mix butter and garlic stock. Place potatoes on a baking dish then brush with butter and garlic. Micro-cook the potatoes uncovered, on high power (100%) for 15–20 minutes. During cooking, baste the potatoes with the butter and garlic stock. When cooked, sprinkle the breadcrumbs over the hot potatoes and add the grated cheese. Reheat 2–4 minutes until the cheese has melted.

If baking in the oven, preheat oven to 200°C and cook for 30–40 minutes, or until the flesh is soft. Add cheese and return to oven until cheese has melted.

Note: Cooking time will vary according to the type of potato.

Bubble and squeak

Quantities depend on the ingredients available and the number of people.

butter or dripping
1 onion, peeled and thinly sliced
cold mashed potatoes
cooked greens of any kind (usually cabbage)
salt and pepper

Fry onion until brown, then add potatoes and greens, and season to taste. Fry until crispy brown, turning frequently.

Variation: Thin slices of cold roast or boiled beef, fried in a little butter or dripping, can be placed on top of the bubble and squeak to make a complete meal.

Potato pizza base

(serves 4)

1 large potato (about 200 g) peeled and grated
4 T grated cheese
2 T wholemeal flour
1 egg, beaten

Preheat oven to 180°C. Mix all ingredients together and bind with egg. Press onto a tray or dish and bake for 20 minutes. Spread with any topping or toppings and bake a further 10 minutes, or until cooked and starting to brown.

Toppings: tomato paste, chopped or sliced onions, peppers, tomatoes, chopped ham, bacon, luncheon meat, salami, cheese, mixed herbs, fresh herbs, sweetcorn, sardines, tuna, shrimps, mushrooms, courgettes, celery, garlic.

Mainly meat

Bosanski ionac (baked pork and vegetables)
(serves 6–8)

This is adapted from an old Yugoslavian recipe. Originally lard was used, but it can be replaced with melted bacon fat or butter.

1 kg boneless pork, thinly sliced, with all fat removed
4 large onions, peeled and thinly sliced
4 large potatoes
4 large peppers, cored and sliced
salt and pepper
paprika
$^{1}/_{2}$ c melted bacon fat or butter
$^{1}/_{2}$ c water
2 c sour cream

Preheat oven to 180°C. Grease a large deep casserole and place half the pork in it. Layer onions, potatoes, peppers and remaining pork into the casserole dish, seasoning the layers with salt, pepper and paprika. Pour over the bacon fat or butter, and water. Spread 1 c of sour cream on top, cover the casserole and bake for 1–1$^{1}/_{4}$ hours.

Spread remaining sour cream on top and place under a hot grill until bubbling and lightly browned. Serve with a fresh green salad.

Opposite: Scalloped potatoes, page 45. (Photograph and recipe courtesy of the New Zealand Vegetable Growers' Federation.)

Cornish pasties

(makes 10–12)

These were traditionally eaten for lunch by the Cornish tin miners. At that time, the filling would have been turnip, potato and a little meat. In this recipe, the proportion of meat to vegetables can be adapted to suit your needs.

Pastry

3 c flour
$^1\!/_2$ t salt
120 g butter
cold water to mix

Filling

4 medium potatoes, peeled and diced
1 small turnip, peeled and chopped
300–400 g beef, chopped
1 small kidney, skinned and chopped (optional)
1 onion, peeled and chopped
1 t salt
2 T tomato sauce
1 egg, beaten

Sift flour, add salt and butter. Using finger tips, rub butter into flour until the mixture is like fine breadcrumbs. Add sufficient cold water to be able to knead the pastry until it is smooth. Chill for 30 minutes. Preheat oven to 200°C. On a lightly floured board, roll out the pastry to about 1–2 cm thickness. Using a small plate, cut the pastry into rounds. (The scraps can be kneaded together and rolled out again.)

In a large bowl, combine potatoes, turnip, beef, kidney, onion, salt and tomato sauce. Place a small amount of filling in the middle of each pastry round. Using a pastry brush, coat the pastry edges with cold water, then join the edges to make a semicircle. With your fingers, press the edges firmly together, and place the pasties on a large baking tray. Using a sharp knife make 2 cuts across the top of each, and brush with beaten egg.

Bake for 35–45 minutes, or until golden brown. Serve with a green salad.

Opposite: Chunky skins, page 45. (Photograph and recipe courtesy of the New Zealand Vegetable Growers' Federation.)

Shepherds' pie

(serves 4–5)

A traditional English dish, using leftover roast meat.

100 g butter
2 medium onions, peeled and minced
750 g–1 kg cooked beef or lamb, diced or finely chopped
1 c gravy (or water and stock cubes)
1–2 T tomato sauce
1–2 t Worcestershire sauce
salt and pepper
500 g cooked mashed potatoes

Preheat oven to 180°C. Melt butter in frying pan, add onions and cook until soft. Add meat to the onion mixture and stir until the meat is lightly browned. Stir in gravy, sauces and seasonings. Heat. Place in a greased casserole dish and cover with mashed potato, using a fork to pattern the top. Bake for 30 minutes, or until well heated and the potato is brown.

Microwaved mutton and kumara stew

(serves 4)

Mutton chops make a tasty meal. Although they take longer to cook than the more expensive cuts, the flavour develops more; and by adding vegetables to the casserole, a substantial meal is ready in 60 minutes with a microwave, or 2–2^1/$_2$ hours if cooked conventionally.

2 T flour
1 t salt
1 t curry powder
1 t black pepper
700–800 g mutton neck chops
1 t oil
2–3 medium carrots, peeled and thinly sliced
1 onion, peeled and sliced
2–3 medium kumara, peeled and chopped
2 stalks celery, peeled and chopped
30 g brown onion sauce mix (or similar)
^{1}/$_2$ c water

Combine flour, salt, curry powder and pepper on a plate or in a plastic bag, and dredge the chops in the seasoned flour. Preheat large casserole-type browning dish for 6–8 minutes in the microwave, then add oil to the dish, then chops. Microwave, uncovered, on high power (100%) for 2 minutes. Turn the chops over and cook a further 2 minutes. Add the vegetables and any remaining seasoned flour.

Combine brown onion sauce mix and water, and pour over the meat and vegetables. Cover the dish and micro-cook for 30 minutes on medium power (50%). Turn chops over and stir vegetables.

Cover and cook for another 30 minutes, or until the meat is tender and the vegetables soft. Stand for 10 minutes before serving.

Irish stew

(serves 5–6)

1 kg mutton neck chops
salt and pepper
2 large onions, peeled and quartered
chopped parsley
1–1.5 kg potatoes, peeled and thickly sliced
2–3 c water

Preheat oven to 180°C. Trim skin and excess fat from chops. Place half of them in the base of a large casserole dish and sprinkle with salt and pepper. Cover with half the onions, parsley, and half the potato slices. Repeat the layers, ending with potato. Season well and add water.

Cover the casserole dish, and bake for 1½ hours before checking to make sure there is enough liquid. Add more water if required. Bake for another 30 minutes uncovered, until the potatoes are browned.

Moussaka (a Greek dish)

(serves 6–8)

2 medium-sized eggplants
2 T oil
50 g butter
750 g minced lamb
1 onion, peeled and sliced
1 T flour
salt and pepper
3 T tomato paste
3 T water
1 clove garlic, peeled and chopped
4 medium potatoes, cooked in their jackets and sliced
4 tomatoes, peeled and sliced
2 T flour
1 c milk
pinch nutmeg
1 egg, beaten
3 T grated tasty cheese

Cut the unpeeled eggplants into 2.5 mm slices, sprinkle with salt, set aside for 30 minutes. Heat oil in frying pan. Drain eggplant slices, dry, and fry until golden brown on both sides. Drain on paper towel. In the frying pan, melt half the butter, add lamb and onion, and cook for 5 minutes. Blend in flour, salt, pepper, tomato paste, water and garlic. Cover and cook slowly for 30 minutes.

Preheat oven to 200°C. In a large greased casserole dish, arrange alternate layers of meat, tomatoes, eggplant and potatoes, adding extra seasoning if required. In a small saucepan, heat remaining butter, add flour, cook for 2 minutes, then gradually add milk and nutmeg. Stir until thick, then slowly add beaten egg and cheese. Spoon the sauce over the casserole. Bake for 20 minutes until thoroughly heated and lightly browned on top.

Peruvian pork stew

(serves 6)

Some years ago we hosted a student from Peru and he cooked this easy-to-make and very nourishing dish. It has been a family favourite ever since.

$^1/_4$ c cooking oil
1 kg pork pieces, trimmed
1 large onion, peeled and sliced
1 t crushed garlic
1–2 t chilli paste (depending on the brand)
1 t cumin seeds, crushed
450-g can whole kernel corn, drained
450-g can peeled chopped tomatoes
1 c orange juice
1 t salt
4 sweet potatoes, peeled and cut into chunks

Heat the cooking oil in a large saucepan, add chopped pork pieces and cook, stirring occasionally, until lightly browned. Transfer the pork to another dish and cover. Add onion, garlic, chilli paste and cumin seeds to the hot saucepan, cook on a moderate heat for 5 minutes, or until the onions are tender. Stir in the corn, tomatoes, orange juice and salt. Bring mixture to the boil, then add pork pieces, reduce heat, cover and simmer for 45 minutes, or until pork is tender.

Boil sweet potatoes in salted water until just tender, then drain. Add to the meat and vegetables. Reheat for a further 10 minutes, adjust seasoning to taste. Serve with a green salad and fresh bread.

Layered sausage casserole

(serves 4–5)

500 g sausage meat
1 large cooking apple, peeled, cored and thinly sliced
1 t mixed herbs
3 bacon rashers, rind removed
2–3 sticks celery, chopped
450 g tomatoes, peeled and sliced
$1^1/_2$–2 c cooked mashed potato
1 c grated tasty cheese

Preheat oven to 180°C. Lightly grease a casserole dish and spread the sausage meat over the base. Place apple on top and sprinkle with the herbs. Layer other ingredients in the order given. Bake for 1 hour.

Potato meat loaf

(serves 8–10 if thinly sliced)

500 g sausage meat
500 g steak mince
1 c fresh breadcrumbs
1 c grated raw potato
1 onion, peeled and finely chopped
1 T curry powder
2 eggs, beaten
1 T chopped parsley
$^1/_2$ t salt
$^1/_2$ c milk

Sauce

$^3/_4$ c water
$^1/_2$ c tomato sauce
$^1/_4$ c Worcestershire sauce
2 T vinegar
1 t instant coffee
2 T lemon juice

Preheat oven to 180°C. Combine all ingredients (except sauce ingredients) and place in a large meat dish. Bake uncovered for 20 minutes, then pour off excess juices. Cover loaf with sauce and bake for 50 minutes.

Sauce: Combine all ingredients in a saucepan and bring to the boil. Simmer for 5 minutes. Stir well and cook for a further 4 minutes. Pour juices reserved from the cooked meat loaf and serve separately. This meat loaf cuts well when hot, but is even better cold the next day. Serve with a tossed salad.

Beef pot roast with vegetables

(serves 4–5)

1 T oil
1–1.5 kg topside roast
$^1/_2$ c water
2 T tomato paste
1 T brown sugar
$^1/_2$ t salt
1 t mixed dried herbs
4 medium potatoes, peeled and sliced
2 large carrots, cut into rings
2 onions, peeled and sliced

Heat oil in a large saucepan, and brown the meat on all sides. Combine water, tomato paste, brown sugar, salt and herbs, pour over meat. Bring to the boil, cover, turn heat to low and simmer for 1 hour. Add vegetables and cook for another hour, or until the meat and vegetables are tender. Spoon juices over the meat and vegetables during cooking, skimming off excess fat if necessary. Slice meat and serve with vegetables. Make gravy, if required, from any leftover juices.

Note: Pork can replace beef but allow 2 hours cooking time before adding the vegetables. Lamb will cook slightly more quickly than beef, depending on the cut and thickness. If this dish is cooked in the oven, allow 2–2$^{1}/_{2}$ hours total cooking time at 160°C for beef.

Beef rolls

(serves 2)

4 slices beef schnitzel
2 t garlic, finely chopped
1 c cooked mashed potato
1 t chopped parsley
2–4 mushrooms, chopped
2 bacon rashers, chopped
salt and pepper
flour
1–2 T butter
$^{1}/_{2}$–1 c red wine
water

Sprinkle beef slices with garlic. Combine potato, parsley, mushrooms, bacon, salt and pepper. Place $^{1}/_{4}$ of the mixture on each slice, roll up and tie with string. Coat rolls with flour. Melt butter in frying pan and lightly brown the rolls. Pour off any excess butter. Stir in wine and sufficient water to just cover the meat. Cover the frying pan and cook gently for 1–1$^{1}/_{2}$ hours.

Note: Alternatively, after browning the rolls, this dish can be placed in a casserole, liquid added, covered and baked at 160°C for 1–1$^{1}/_{2}$ hours.

Beef and lentil casserole

(serves 4)

This recipe uses only a small amount of beef. Use red or brown lentils; the quantities for vegetables are only a guide.

100 g lentils (washed and soaked overnight)
6–8 c water
100 g stewing steak
2 carrots, peeled and diced
1 turnip or swede, peeled and diced
2 onions, peeled and chopped
3–4 medium potatoes, thinly sliced
salt and pepper

Preheat oven to 180°C. Place lentils in a large saucepan, add 6–8 c of water, bring to the boil and simmer for 10 minutes. Drain, but reserve water. Cut the meat into small pieces and place in a greased casserole dish. Cover with lentils and 2–3 cups of reserved water. Add carrots, turnip and onions, making sure the water comes halfway up the dish. Overlap the slices of potato on top. Cover the casserole and bake for 1³/₄ hours. Uncover, add seasonings, and bake for a further 15–25 minutes to brown the potatoes.

Potato beef goulash

(serves 3–4)

2 T cooking oil
2 onions, peeled and sliced
1 T paprika
500 g chuck steak, cut into thin strips
1 T flour
1 c water
1 T tomato purée
salt
1 t vinegar
¹/₂–1 t dried marjoram
3–4 medium potatoes, peeled and sliced

Preheat oven to 170°C. Heat cooking oil in large frying pan, add onions and cook until golden brown. Add paprika and stir well. Roll meat in flour and add to the frying pan. Stir well and cook for 5 minutes. Add water, tomato purée, salt, vinegar and marjoram. Stir until well mixed and simmering. Place half the potatoes in a greased casserole dish. Add the meat and liquid. Top with remaining slices of potato. Cover the casserole and cook for 2 hours. Remove the lid and continue cooking for 20–25 minutes until the potatoes are crisp and brown.

Veal, potato and apple casserole

(serves 4)

Veal is sometimes in short supply, but thinly sliced beef or pork may be substituted.

500 g lean stewing veal, diced
2 T flour
salt and pepper
1 T butter
1 onion, peeled and sliced
2–3 medium potatoes, peeled and sliced
2 large cooking apples, peeled, cored and thinly sliced
1 t sugar
1 t mixed herbs
1 c chicken stock (or water and stock cube)
$^1/_2$ c sour cream

Preheat oven to 170°C. Roll meat in flour, salt and pepper until well covered. Melt butter in frying pan, brown meat, then add onions and cook for 2–3 minutes. Place potatoes in casserole dish and top with meat and onions. Add apples (reserving 3–4 slices for garnishing.) Sprinkle with sugar and herbs, then gently pour stock over mixture. Cover and cook slowly for 1½ hours. Just before serving, spoon on the sour cream, stir, adjust seasoning and garnish with apple slices.

Pork and apple pie

(serves 4)

Potato pastry

1 large potato, cooked and grated
1 c flour
1 t baking powder
50 g butter
water to mix

Filling

700–800 g cubed pork pieces
2 cooking apples, peeled, cored and chopped
1 T sugar
1 small onion, peeled and grated
½ c water
salt and pepper

Pastry: Preheat oven to 200°C. Combine potato, sifted flour and baking powder. Rub in butter, then add sufficient water to form a stiff dough. Roll out to fit on top of a casserole dish.

Filling: Place a layer of pork in a deep, greased casserole dish. Add a layer of apples. Sprinkle with sugar, and layer the meat and apples again. Place the grated onion on the top layer. Press down well and add water, salt and pepper.

Top with pastry, flute edges and seal against the casserole dish edge. Bake for 10–15 minutes, then reduce heat to 160°C and bake for another 45 minutes.

Apple sausages and potato topping

(serves 4–6)

1 T oil
1 large onion, peeled and sliced
750–800 g pork sausages, skinned
2 T flour
salt and pepper
1 t dried mixed herbs
1 large cooking apple, peeled, cored and chopped
1 c apple juice

Topping

30–40 g melted butter
2–3 c hot mashed potato
¹/₂–1 c grated tasty cheese
4 tomatoes, sliced

Preheat oven to 180°C. Heat oil in frying pan and fry onion until tender. Remove onion from pan and set aside. Roll sausages in flour, salt and pepper, then fry in oil until golden brown. Pour off any excess fat. Add herbs, apple, juice and cooked onions, stir well and simmer for 5 minutes. Transfer contents of frying pan to a casserole dish.

Beat melted butter and mashed potato together until smooth. Spoon on top of the sausages and pattern with a fork. Sprinkle with cheese. Bake in oven for 20 minutes. Remove, and place sliced tomatoes around the outer edge of the potato. Return to oven and cook until the tomatoes are just heated and the potato top is golden brown.

Fisherman's pie

(serves 3–4)

1 T butter
1 small onion, peeled and chopped
1 T flour
2 c milk
310 g canned fish, drained
2 eggs, hardboiled and sliced
1–2 cups cold mashed potatoes
¹/₂–1 c grated tasty cheese
1–2 tomatoes, sliced

Preheat oven to 180°C. Melt butter in a saucepan, add onion and cook until tender. Stir in flour and cook for 1–2 minutes. Gradually add milk and stir until thick. Gently add fish and heat. Pour into a greased pie dish, add eggs, and top with a layer of mashed potato.

Sprinkle grated cheese on top. Bake for 20 minutes, or until the cheese melts. Add slices of tomato and return to the oven for 5–8 minutes. Serve with a green tossed salad.

Note: For extra flavour, add ¹/₂ t curry powder with the chopped onion.

Black-eye pea casserole

(serves 4–5)

Soak the black-eye peas for at least 1 hour before preparing the rest of the casserole. Vegetables can be prepared while the peas are cooking. The amounts of vegetables used are a guide only; they can be chopped or diced.

2 c black-eye peas
3 c water
3 T oil or butter
1 large onion, chopped or diced
2 cloves of garlic
3 large potatoes, chopped or diced
1 turnip, chopped or diced
2 carrots, chopped or diced
3 celery sticks, chopped or diced
1 T chopped fresh parsley
1 bay leaf
1 t dried oregano
1 t salt
1 t treacle
2 T tomato purée or paste
1 c grated cheddar cheese

After soaking, place peas and the water in which they were soaked in a large saucepan, bring to boil, and boil for 10 minutes. Cover, and simmer for another 20 minutes, or until the peas are tender. Preheat oven to 180°C. Meanwhile, heat oil or butter in a frying pan, add onion and garlic, and fry until nearly soft. Stir in the potatoes, turnip, carrots, and celery. Cover and cook for 10 minutes. Drain the peas, reserving the liquid. Transfer vegetables to a casserole, adding peas, parsley, bay leaf, oregano and salt. Pour on the reserved liquid (making it up to 3–4 c with extra water, to ensure the vegetables are just covered). Stir in the treacle and tomato purée. Cover tightly and cook for 1½ hours, then discard bay leaf, sprinkle with grated cheese and cook without the lid for 10 minutes. This allows the cheese to melt and the juices in the casserole to evaporate making it thicken slightly.

Fish and potato savouries

(makes 8–16, depending on size)

Smoked or canned fish can be used. Adjust the amount of chilli paste or sauce according to how spicy you like your food.

250–350 g smoked fish, flaked
25 g butter
1 small onion, peeled and chopped
2 medium potatoes, cooked and sieved
1 t tomato sauce
2–3 drops Tabasco sauce
salt and pepper
1 egg, beaten
dried breadcrumbs
oil for shallow frying
1 c tomato purée (or 1 c water and 2 t tomato paste)
$^1/_2$ t chilli paste or sauce

Check fish to make sure all bones have been removed. In a small saucepan, melt the butter, add onion and cook until just tender. Add potatoes, tomato sauce and Tabasco, salt and pepper. Mix well. Using floured hands, shape the mixture into small balls, dip in beaten egg, then roll in breadcrumbs and put in the refrigerator to set for at least 1 hour.

Heat oil in frying pan and fry fish balls until golden brown all over. Drain on paper towel to remove any excess oil, and keep warm. Heat tomato purée, add chilli paste, stir well, and serve in a small bowl with the fish balls.

If serving with pre-dinner drinks, skewer each fish ball with a toothpick for easy dipping. As an entrée, place 3–4 fishballs on a small plate, with 2–3 T of sauce.

Porky snacks

(serves 3–4)

4–6 large pork sausages
tomato sauce or sweet pickle
2–3 c cooked mashed potato

Grill or fry sausages, cool slightly, then split open lengthwise. Spread with tomato sauce or pickle. Spoon mashed potato into a forcing bag and pipe onto the sausage. Place under a hot grill and cook until golden brown.

Potato and bacon tart

(serves 6–8)

When making a pastry base, do not add too much water when combining the ingredients, as this will cause shrinkage. There is no need to pre-bake this base.

Pastry

2 c flour
150 g butter
1 egg
$^1/_4$–$^1/_2$ c cold water

Filling

1 onion, peeled and chopped
1 potato, boiled and grated
2–3 T dried bacon bits
1 c milk
1 c cream
2 eggs
2 T flour
salt and pepper
chopped parsley or chives

Combine pastry ingredients and mix quickly in a food processor until a ball is formed. On a floured board, roll out to fit a 27-cm quiche dish. (Wrapping the pastry around a rolling pin makes it easier to transfer from board to dish.) Line the dish, but do not prick the pastry.

Preheat oven to 190°C. Sprinkle the onion, potato and bacon bits on the pastry. Mix together milk, cream, eggs and flour, and pour over the vegetables. Sprinkle with salt and pepper, top with parsley or chives. Bake for 40–45 minutes, or until set and golden brown.

Family tea slice

(serves 2–3)

1 sheet ready-rolled flakey pastry
2 t mustard sauce or tomato chutney
1 c chopped ham, bacon or similar
1 c mashed potato
3 eggs, beaten
1 small onion, peeled and finely chopped
1 c tasty grated cheese
salt and pepper
milk if required

Preheat oven to 180°C. Line a sponge roll tin with flakey pastry and spread with mustard sauce. Combine other ingredients (only adding milk if potato is very dry). Spread mixture over the sauce and pastry. Bake for 25 minutes, or until golden brown. Cut into fingers and serve.

Fish cakes

(makes 6–8)

500 g fish fillets, cooked
2 c mashed potato
1 T chopped parsley
2 T grated lemon rind
$^1\!/_2$–1 t dry mustard
salt and pepper
2 eggs, beaten
2 T milk
flour and dried breadcrumbs
cooking oil for frying
lemon wedges and parsley (for garnish)

Skin, bone and flake fish fillets. Mix with potato, parsley, lemon rind, mustard, salt, pepper and one beaten egg. Form into 6 or 8 round patties. Combine other egg and milk. Dip fish patties into flour, then egg mixture and finally breadcrumbs. Set in refrigerator for 45–60 minutes.

Heat cooking oil and deep fry fish patties until golden brown. Drain on paper towels. Serve very hot garnished with lemon wedges and sprigs of parsley.

Quick seafood pie

(serves.4–5)

Use cooked chopped mussels, pipis, tuatua, or any other seafood, but be careful not to overcook them.

6 T butter
1 small onion, peeled and finely chopped
2 c cooked diced potatoes
2 c cooked chopped mussels
salt and pepper
chopped parsley
$\frac{1}{2}$ c cream

Melt butter in frying pan and sauté onion until soft. Add potatoes, mussels, salt and pepper. Spread mixture evenly in the frying pan and cook over a medium heat for 10 minutes. Pour cream over the hot mixture, sprinkle with chopped parsley and cook for another 10 minutes. Preheat grill. Place the mixture under it and grill until the cream has set and the top is golden brown. Cut and serve.

Wholemeal vegetable samosas

(makes 12–15)

These samosas are baked instead of deep frying. They are ideal served with pre-dinner drinks, part of the picnic food, or as a starter before a spicy main course. White flour can be substituted for wholemeal. Use silverbeet if spinach is not available. Adjust the spices to suit your palette.

3 carrots, peeled and diced
4 potatoes, peeled and diced
$\frac{1}{2}$ t salt
$\frac{1}{2}$ t cumin seeds
$\frac{1}{2}$ t coriander seeds
1 t ground turmeric
$\frac{1}{4}$ t chilli powder
1 c boiling water
1 c.frozen peas (optional)
4–5 spinach leaves, finely chopped

Pastry

3 c self-raising flour
75 g butter
cold water to mix
extra flour
milk

Preheat oven to 200°C. In a medium-sized saucepan, put carrots, potatoes, salt, cumin, coriander, turmeric, chilli powder and boiling water. Cover tightly and simmer for 10 minutes. Shake the saucepan occasionally to prevent the vegetables from sticking. Add peas and spinach (extra water may be required) and simmer for 5 minutes. Remove lid and allow to cool while making the pastry.

Pastry: Sift flour, rub in butter and add water to make a soft dough. Dust board with flour and roll out pastry thinly. Cut into squares approximately 8 x 8 cm. Place a teaspoon of the vegetable mixture in the centre of each square. Fold the pastry over to form a triangle, using a little milk to moisten the edges. Press edges together with fork or fingers. Place samosas on a greased baking tray and bake for 20–25 minutes, or until golden brown.

Colonial goulash

(serves 4)

1 c haricot beans (soaked in cold water overnight)
1 c barley (soaked in cold water overnight)
3–4 mutton shanks, cut in half
8 c water
1 T salt
2 kumara, peeled and chopped
2–3 potatoes, peeled and chopped
carrots, parsnip, turnip, celery, peeled and chopped
1 T soy sauce
1 T paprika
2 c tomato soup

Drain beans and barley and place in a large saucepan with mutton shanks, water and salt. Cover and simmer for 1 hour, skimming off any fat that rises to the surface. Add vegetables, soy sauce, paprika and tomato soup. Simmer for 30 minutes, or until the vegetables are cooked. Thicken only if required. Season to taste, and serve.

Note: Rice or lentils (soaked overnight), can be used instead of beans and barley; or a small quantity of each. The vegetables given are a guide only.

Vegetable stockpot

(serves 8–10)

The vegetables listed are only a guide. Do not overcook or mash them as it is the variety of colour and shape that makes this dish so appealing.

25 g butter
10–15 baby potatoes (or 3 medium, cut into chunks)
500 g pumpkin, peeled, seeded and cubed
1 large onion, peeled and sliced
3 carrots, peeled and sliced
1 medium turnip, peeled and diced
1–2 sweet potato (or kumara), peeled and cut into chunks
4 sticks celery
1 T tomato paste
8 c chicken stock (or water and stock cubes)
1 T salt
1 c pasta shapes
4–5 leaves silverbeet, shredded
1 c green beans or peas (fresh or frozen)
1 c grated tasty cheese (for garnish)
3–4 T chopped parsley (for garnish)

Melt butter in large stockpot, add potatoes, pumpkin, onion, carrots, turnip, sweet potato and celery. Sauté for 5–10 minutes, stir in tomato paste, then add stock and salt. Bring to the boil, cover and simmer for 30 minutes, or until vegetables are almost tender. Increase heat, add pasta, silverbeet and peas, cook for 10–15 minutes until pasta is soft, stirring occasionally. (Remove the lid to reduce liquid if desired.) Adjust seasonings. Ladle into serving bowls and sprinkle with cheese and parsley.

Note: 3–4 T bacon bits can be added with the stock for a meaty flavour if required.

Chicken and bacon casserole

(serves 6)

3 bacon rashers
6 chicken quarters
2 T flour
salt and pepper
1 large onion, peeled and sliced
1 c sliced mushrooms
2–3 tomatoes, peeled and chopped
½ c white wine
1 t salt
1 c water
1 T chopped fresh herbs
4 medium potatoes, peeled and thickly sliced

Preheat oven to 160°C. Fry bacon until crisp and chop into small pieces. Roll chicken pieces in combined flour, salt and pepper, and brown in the bacon fat. Place chicken and bacon in an ovenproof casserole dish. Fry the onion in the bacon fat and add to the casserole. Add mushrooms, tomatoes, wine, salt, water and herbs. Adjust seasoning. Thicken sauce if necessary by combining 1 T cornflour and 2 T water, and stirring into the hot sauce. Place the potatoes slices on top, then cover the casserole and bake for 1½ hours, or until the meat is tender and the potatoes are soft. Brown for 3–5 minutes under the grill, or uncover, increase the oven heat, and bake until the potatoes are golden brown.

Duck and potato roulade

(serves 5–6)

Wild ducks tend to be very small, so this recipe uses a combination of duck and potato.

2 T butter
1 onion, peeled and chopped
1 T flour
1 t curry powder (or mustard)
2 oranges, juice and rind
½ c water
3–4 c cooked, chopped duck meat or similar
2 T sweet pickle or chutney
3–4 T dry breadcrumbs
1 kg potato, cooked and mashed
parsley and orange slices (for garnish)

Preheat oven to 180°C. Melt butter in a frying pan, add onion and cook until tender. Add flour and curry powder, cook for 2 minutes, then stir in orange juice and rind with water. Stir well, cooking for 3–4 minutes until thickened. Add chopped duck meat and pickle. Spread breadcrumbs over a large cut-open oven bag, and cover with mashed potato, making an even square shape. Add the duck. Gently lift the ends of the oven bag and partly roll the potato away from you. Lift the far side, partly roll towards you, so that the potato nearly joins in the middle. Do not try to overlap. Using the oven bag as support, lift the potato roll and place seam side down on an ovenproof dish.

Bake for 30–40 minutes until firm and browned. Garnish with parsley and orange slices.

Note: Ham, chopped turkey or chicken can be used as a filling. Adjust seasoning to taste. Finely chopped sautéed red and green peppers may be added to the potato for colour and texture.

Home-cooked fish and chips

Chips: Older potatoes make better chips. Peel and cut the potatoes into thick slices, and then cut these slices into strips, about 1 cm wide. Soak the chips in cold water for at least 30 minutes to remove any starch. Preheat a deep fryer or a deep saucepan that is half-filled with cooking oil.

Dry the potato chips and, using a wire basket, slowly lower about a cup of chips into the oil. (To test whether the oil is hot enough, drop in a chip and, if it rises to the surface immediately and is surrounded by bubbles, the oil is at the right temperature. Do not attempt to cook too many chips at once or it will lower the cooking temperature of the oil which will then soak into the chips.)

Cook for 6–10 minutes, depending on the heat and the type of oil used. When the chips are brown, drain and place on a paper towel. Repeat the process with the remaining chips. Just prior to serving, fry all the chips again in batches. Drain and serve sprinkled with salt and pepper.

Fish batter (1)

2 c flour
2 eggs, separated
1 c beer
pinch of salt
2 T melted butter

Sift the flour into a bowl, add egg yolks and beer. Whisk until smooth. Stir in the salt and melted butter. Stand covered for 30 minutes. Whisk egg whites until stiff, and carefully fold into the batter. Coat fish fillets in extra flour, then dip into the batter, and fry until the fish is golden brown on both sides.

Fish batter (2)

1 egg
1 c cold water
1 c flour
1 t baking powder
$^1/_2$ t salt

Beat egg with water, add the dry ingredients, adding extra water if needed to make the batter a thick, creamy consistency. Cook as above.

Toppings for meat pies

Potato savoury pastry (to fit a 20-cm dish)

50 g butter
1 c flour
1$^1/_2$ c mashed potato
1 t baking powder
1 t green herb stock or small minced onion
milk to mix

Rub butter into flour, add potato, baking powder, stock and sufficient milk to make a stiff dough. Roll out and use on top of hot meat, fish or vegetable pies. Bake at 200°C for 10 minutes, then reduce heat to 180°C and bake for a further 15–20 minutes until pastry is well risen and browned.
Note: The pastry will be lighter if placed over very hot meat.

Vegetable Topping (to fit a 20-cm dish)

1–2 carrots, peeled and grated
1 parsnip or turnip, peeled and grated
2 T butter, melted
1–2 c mashed potato
salt and pepper

Combine carrots and parsnip or turnip. Add butter to mashed potato and beat well, adding seasoning if necessary. Combine mixtures, and spoon over the meat. Pattern the top with a fork. Bake at 180°C for 30–40 minutes, or until golden.

Baking (bread, cakes, desserts, etc.)

Chocolate potato cake

The mashed sieved potato keeps the cake moist. This recipe can be halved, but shorten the cooking time to 25–30 minutes.

250 g butter
1¹/₂ c sugar
2 c mashed potato, sieved
4 eggs, beaten
2 c flour
4 t baking powder
2 T cocoa
¹/₂ t salt
¹/₂ c milk

Preheat oven to 190°C. Line a 30 x 30-cm baking tin with greaseproof paper. Cream butter and sugar, add potato and mix to a smooth paste. Stir in beaten eggs. Sift flour, baking powder, cocoa and salt, add to creamed ingredients. Stir in milk to make a soft mixture that can easily be spooned into the lined baking tin. Smooth the top.

Bake for 45–60 minutes, or until the top of the cake is firm and, when a skewer is inserted in the middle, it comes out cleanly. Leave to stand for 5 minutes, then turn onto a rack and leave to cool.

Ice with peppermint flavoured chocolate icing or cut the cake in half and fill with whipped or mock cream. Dust the top with icing sugar.

Coffee and coconut biscuits

(makes 20–25)

1 c mashed potato, sieved
100 g butter
³/₄ c sugar
2 eggs
1¹/₂ c self-raising flour
¹/₂ c coconut
1 T instant coffee
2 T boiling water

Preheat oven to 180°C. Cream together potato, butter and sugar until well blended. Beat eggs and add to creamed mixture. Stir in flour and coconut. Dissolve the instant coffee in the boiling water, add to the mixture and stir well. Roll into balls, about the size of a 20 cent coin. If too wet to handle easily, add a little extra flour. Place well-spaced on a cold oven tray and press down firmly with a fork.

Bake 15–20 minutes until golden brown. Cool on a wire rack before storing in an airtight container.

Tasty cheese muffins

(makes 12)

2 c flour
3 t baking powder
¹/₂–1 t curry powder
1 c grated tasty cheese
200 g cooked and grated potato
50 g butter, melted
³/₄ c milk
2 eggs, beaten
2 bacon rashers, cooked and finely chopped

Preheat oven to 220°C. Sift flour, baking powder and curry powder together. Using a knife, mix in the cheese and potato. Combine the butter, milk and eggs, and stir into the dry ingredients. Add chopped bacon. Do not overmix. Spoon the moist mixture into 12 patty pans.

Bake for 12–15 minutes, then leave to stand for 3–5 minutes before removing from the pans. Serve warm or cold. Cut and spread with butter and jam, top with extra slices of cheese, or leave plain and serve with hot soup.

Almond and passionfruit tart

(serves 8–10)

Potato pastry

1½ c flour
2 t baking powder
½ c mashed potato, sieved
pinch salt
150 g butter
cold water
2 T raspberry jam

Filling

1 c mashed potato, sieved
100 g butter
½ c sugar
4 eggs
100 g ground almonds
½ c passionfruit pulp

Preheat oven to 190°C. Combine flour, baking powder, potato and salt in a bowl. Cut in the butter and add sufficient water to make a soft dough. Roll out or press into a 25-cm springbase (or loose based) pie dish or baking tin, allowing for 5–10 cm to form the side crust. Place pie shell in fridge for at least 15 minutes. Spread base with raspberry jam.

Filling: Cream potato, butter and sugar, add eggs and beat well. Stir in the almonds and passionfruit pulp. Pour mixture into pastry shell and bake for 45–60 minutes, or until firm and set, reducing the temperature if it browns too quickly. Cut into wedges and serve with whipped cream or icecream.

Savoury potato biscuits

(makes 20–30)

These biscuits are delicious with dips, as pre-dinner nibbles, or topped with a savoury spread.

1 c rolled oats
1 c flour
50 g butter
1 c mashed potato
½ c grated tasty cheese
½ t salt
milk if required
extra flour

Preheat oven to 180°C. Combine rolled oats and flour, then rub in the butter. Mix in the mashed potato, cheese and salt. Add milk if required, to make a stiff dough. Sprinkle extra flour on a board and roll out the dough thinly, then cut into squares, strips or circles. Re-mix any leftover dough, roll out again and cut, until all the dough is used. Place the shapes onto a lightly greased tray and bake for 15–20 minutes until crisp and brown. Store in an airtight container.

Savoury kumara loaf

(serves 3–4)

1 c cooked and mashed kumara
2 c minced cold meat
1 small onion, peeled and minced
1 apple, peeled, cored and grated
1–2 T chopped parsley
2 T pickle
1 egg, beaten
salt and pepper

Preheat oven to 180°C. Combine all ingredients and spoon into greased loaf tin. Bake for 40–60 minutes. Stand covered for 10 miniutes, then turn out and slice.

Fruit-topped baked cheesecake

(serves 6–8)

Fresh or canned fruit can be used as a topping on this cheesecake. The addition of potato with the cream cheese increases the volume of the filling, and makes the desert extremely easy to cut and serve.

1 sheet ready-rolled flakey pastry
250 g cream cheese, Quark or ricotta cheese
4 eggs
$\frac{1}{2}$ c sugar
1 t vanilla essence
1 c cold mashed potato, sieved
$\frac{1}{2}$–1 c fresh or canned fruit (including juice)
1 t gelatine
2 T boiling water

Preheat oven to 150°C. Line base of a 20 x 20-cm cake tin with the flakey pastry. In a bowl combine cream cheese, eggs, sugar, vanilla essence and potato. Beat or whisk until smooth. Pour mixture into the pastry shell. Bake 40–60 minutes, or until well-risen and set. Remove from the oven and cool.

Topping: Depending on the fruit used, purée or chop as required. Combine gelatine with boiling water and stir until it is dissolved, then add to the fresh fruit and juice. Pour the fruit mixture over the cooled cheesecake. Place in refrigerator until the topping has set. Cut into serving portions and top with whipped cream if desired.

Potato bread

(makes 1 large or 2 medium loaves, or 20 rolls)

3 T granulated yeast
4 c warm water
1 t sugar
8–9 c flour (white, wholemeal, or a combination)
2 t salt
3 medium cooked potatoes, mashed or grated
extra flour and warm water as required
1 egg yolk
1 T water
poppy seeds, sesame seeds, grated cheese, bacon pieces

Combine yeast, water and sugar in a bowl, set aside for 10 minutes, or until frothy. Sift flour and salt into a large mixing bowl, add potato, stir well. Pour the yeast mixture into the flour and knead to a soft dough. Add extra flour or warm water as required (different types of flour will absorb different quantities of liquid). When the dough is smooth, place in the mixing bowl, cover and leave in a warm place to rise until doubled in size. Knead the dough again, and mould into 2 loaves, plait into one large loaf, or shape into 20 small rolls.

Leave in a warm place to rise again for 20–30 minutes. Preheat oven to 200°C. Combine egg yolk with water and brush over the bread or rolls. Sprinkle with seeds, cheese and/or bacon. Bake for 25 minutes for rolls, 45–60 minutes for the bread, depending on the size. Check after 20 minutes and reduce to 180°C if browning too quickly. The bread is cooked if, when you tap it, it has a hollow sound. Leave to cool, then slice as required.

Baking powder bread

(makes 1 loaf)

This bread is made more quickly than the recipe using yeast, but it does not keep so well. It should be eaten the day it is cooked.

4 c flour
1 t salt
1 t sugar
4 t baking powder
1 medium potato, cooked and grated or sieved
2½–3 c milk
melted butter

Preheat oven to 220°C. Sift together flour, salt, sugar and baking powder and then rub in potato. Add sufficient milk to make a soft dough. Knead lightly, then place in a greased loaf tin. Brush the top with warm milk or melted butter. Bake for 35–45 minutes. Allow to stand for 5 minutes, then turn out and slice when cold.

Christmas plum pudding

(serves 6–8)

At one time, Christmas puddings were always cooked well in advance, so they could mature. They were cooked in a floured cloth and boiled in "coppers", as there were no saucepans large enough to take the pudding. The addition of vegetables and stout to this recipe adds flavour and texture.

6 c mixed dried fruit
1 c shredded suet
1 c fresh breadcrumbs
1 c brown sugar
2 large carrots, peeled and grated
2 large potatoes, peeled and grated
1 c flour
$^{1}/_{2}$ c chopped almonds
$^{1}/_{2}$ c stout, ale or water
2 t each of nutmeg, cinnamon, ginger, mixed spice

Combine all ingredients. (A large preserving pan or stock pot is ideal.) Grease a 2.5-litre aluminium or crockery bowl and spoon in 8 c of mixture. Cover the bowl with a double sheet of greaseproof paper, with a pleat in it. (This allows for the swelling of the pudding.) Tie the paper down tightly. Lower the bowl into the saucepan of boiling water, ensuring that the water reaches halfway up the bowl. Boil for 6 hours. Check frequently, and add more boiling water as necessary to maintain the water level. The remaining puddings can be cooked in 4–5 c lots, steaming each for 4 hours. Freeze until required. Defrost slowly. To reheat, steam the large pudding for another 2 hours; smaller puddings 1 hour each.

Baked fruit sponge

(serves 5–6)
Any fruit can be used but make sure it is bubbling when adding the topping; this ensures a light sponge finish.

150 g butter
$^1/_2$ c brown sugar
1 medium potato, boiled and sieved
1 T golden syrup
2 eggs
1 c self-raising flour
2 t ground ginger
1–2 T glacé ginger, finely chopped
3–4 c hot stewed fruit

Preheat oven to 200°C. Cream butter, sugar, potato and golden syrup until well blended. Add eggs and beat again. Sift in flour and ground ginger, stir, then add glacé ginger. Place bubbling stewed fruit in a casserole dish and spoon over the sponge mixture. Bake for 35–45 minutes, reducing temperature to 180°C after 15 minutes. Sponge should be golden brown and well risen. Serve with cream or a light custard.

For variation: omit glacé ginger; cinnamon and nutmeg can be used instead of ground ginger. Combining small amounts of different fruits can make an interesting base. Try rhubarb and apple, apple and blackberry, raspberry and apple, or peaches or nectarines with passionfruit pulp.

Lemon loaf

150 g soft butter
$^3/_4$ c sugar
200 g cooked grated potato
2 eggs
2 large lemons
2 c self-raising flour
1 T sugar

Preheat oven to 180°C. Combine butter, sugar and potato, and beat until smooth. Add eggs, the juice and grated rind of 1 lemon, and stir in the flour. Spoon into a greased loaf tin. Bake 30–40 minutes until risen and golden brown. Remove from oven and leave to stand for 5 minutes. Remove loaf from tin, and stand on a cake rack. Pierce with a skewer, and pour the juice of the other lemon over it. Sprinkle with sugar. Leave to stand until completely cold. Slice as needed.

Note: If preferred, omit extra lemon juice, and ice with lemon butter icing, using grated lemon rind sprinkled on the icing for taste and effect.

Potato scones

(makes 8–10)

Slightly heavier in texture than traditional scones, these are excellent for breakfast, served with bacon and eggs.

2 c self-raising flour
1 t baking powder
¹/₂ t salt
¹/₂ t curry powder
1 c cooked, sieved potato
100 g butter, melted
¹/₂–³/₄ c milk

Preheat oven to 200°C. Sift flour, baking powder, salt and curry powder, and add potato. Combine butter and ¹/₂ c milk, add to flour mix to make a firm dough, adding extra milk as required. Pat into a circle and cut into 8 triangular shapes. Place on a heated tray, keeping the circle shape, but spacing each triangle slightly apart. (This allows for even baking). Bake for 12–15 minutes until well risen and browned.

Sally Lunn

¹/₂ c sultanas
1 c water
1 c cold mashed potato
1 c sugar
2 c self-raising flour
2 c milk
1 c icing sugar
1 t butter
2–3 drops cochineal (red food colouring)
hot water to mix
1–2 T coconut

Preheat oven to 180°C. Combine sultanas and water in a small saucepan and boil for 5–6 minutes. Drain and cool. Beat the potato and sugar together (the mixture will be very wet). Add sultanas, flour, and enough milk to make a moist batter. Spoon the mixture onto a greased oven tray and bake for 30–35 minutes or until golden brown. Cool.

Icing: Combine icing sugar, butter, cochineal and enough boiling water to make a firm icing. Spoon on to the loaf, smooth with a knife and sprinkle with coconut. Slice when cold. Butter as desired.

Index